Start Your Own Woodworking Business

Profit from your passion!

Norman Pirollo

The terms **furniture, cabinets, wood products** can be used interchangeably in this course. The goal here is to discuss the woodworking products you intend to produce and market.

Wood products can include wood crafts, small items such as birdhouses, carvings, wood sculptures, outdoor furniture, turned products such as pens or candle holders, bowls, furniture, etc.

No part of this book may be reproduced or transmitted in any form by any means, graphic, electronic, or mechanical, including photocopying, recording, taping or by any information retrieval system, without permission in writing from the author.

Warning and Disclaimer: The information in this book is offered with the understanding that it does not contain legal, financial, or other professional advice. Individuals requiring such services should consult a competent professional. The author and publisher make no representations about the suitability of the information contained in this book for any purpose. The material is provided "as is" without warranty of any kind. Although every effort has been made to ensure the accuracy of the contents of this book, errors and omissions can occur. The author and publisher assume no responsibility for any damages arising from the use of this book or alleged to have resulted in connection with this book. This book is not completely comprehensive. Some readers may wish to consult additional books for advice.

Author: Norman Pirollo
All rights reserved | Tous droits réservés
© 2022 WoodSkills, Pirollo Design
Ottawa, Ontario ON K0A 2P0 CANADA

Contents

INTRODUCTION 1

IS SELF-EMPLOYMENT FOR YOU? 3

CONVERTING A HOBBY INTO A BUSINESS? 13
Important questions to ask yourself 13

EXPANDING ON QUESTIONS YOU NEED TO ASK YOURSELF 17
Have you successfully made furniture or cabinets before? 17
Are you comfortable dealing with clients? 18
Are you familiar with the joinery used in making furniture and cabinets? 18
How skilled are you at applying finishes to woodworking projects? 23
How long does it take you to make wood products, furniture or cabinets? 26
Are you capable of working within deadlines? 28
Can you handle business that detracts from woodworking? 28
Part Time vs. Full Time? 29

FINDING OR CREATING A NICHE FOR YOUR WOODWORKING 35

LEGAL CONSIDERATIONS 39

A BUSINESS PLAN 43

WHAT EQUIPMENT AND TOOLS DO I NEED? 45

HOW MUCH SPACE DO I NEED? 57

DEVELOPING A PRODUCT OR PRODUCTS 61

CREATING OR FINDING A MARKET FOR YOUR WORK 71

CREATING A PORTFOLIO OF YOUR WORK 75

INTERNET MARKETING 79

COPING WITH THE UPS AND DOWNS OF A BUSINESS 81

MAINTAINING BALANCE BETWEEN BUSINESS AND PERSONAL LIFE 83

MAINTAINING THE PASSION AND MOTIVATION 85

CREATING EXCELLENT CLIENT RELATIONSHIPS 87

MAKING FURNITURE AND WOOD PRODUCTS ON COMMISSION ... 89

DIVERSIFYING AND EXPANDING 93

CONSIDERATIONS TO EXPAND A BUSINESS 95

Do you have the space for a larger business? 95

Will there be a market for your business expansion? 98

Do you need to create a larger market for your wood products? 99

Are you able to handle the extra business? 99

How does an expansion work within your present location? 100

Do you need to hire an employee? 105

TECHNOLOGY IN WOODWORKING 111

SOCIAL MEDIA FOR WOODWORKERS 117

CONCLUSION 129

Introduction

I have written this book to share my experience with starting a business, specifically a woodworking business. Initially, I began two part-time woodworking companies while working at a day job. This was done to minimize the risk of losing my regular income. The regular income also helped finance the tools and equipment necessary to get the businesses going. Once established, it was found that I spent as much time working at my business than at my day job.

It was at this juncture that the decision was made to let go of my day job and focus entirely on the woodworking business. My business volume has progressed rapidly since then and I have never looked back. Being self-employed brings great satisfaction and fulfillment to my life. Being able to work at something I genuinely enjoy has brought me success and a rewarding career.

I also owe gratitude to a supportive family. It is important to have a spouse or partner that supports the fact that you will be going into business for yourself. There is a considerable amount to learn about self-employment which demands time and effort. Hopefully, this book will answer many questions you might have and address any doubts you have about being self-employed at a woodworking business.

It should also be mentioned of the importance in creating a business plan and following it. A business plan will outline the steps you need to follow to make your woodworking business a success. A business plan will also serve to steer you back when it is felt you have veered into a different direction. It is easy to lose focus in a woodworking business and accept work which does not help with the success of your business.

Sincerely,

Norman Pirollo

Is Self-Employment for You?

The following assumes you have developed a passion for woodworking and often give thought to striking out on your own as a woodworker. How often have you wondered or dreamt about earning a living from your woodworking passion? Maybe you are currently in a rut with your existing career, not deriving much satisfaction from your current job, or out of work. There are many reasons why people dream about working at something they enjoy. The thought of spending hours designing and creating tangible products is a source of great satisfaction for many people. Many people enjoy the creative aspect of life.

To be able to create furniture, cabinets or wood objects can be greatly appealing. Doing this for a living, either part-time or full-time, can be rewarding and satisfying. Having started and developed four of my own woodworking businesses, I can attest to the excitement of watching a business grow. If the business revolves around something you enjoy doing, success is almost guaranteed. In the latter years of my woodworking career, I have also begun teaching and creating woodworking tutorials, plans and woodworking courses through WoodSkills. This allows me the privilege to share the knowledge and expertise I have gained over the years.

I very much support individuals going into business for themselves and encourage this at every opportunity. Writing this book allows me to share my experiences in starting a woodworking business.

Norman Pirollo

One of the woodworking businesses developed by the author, Refined Edge Design.

WoodSkills Instructional Woodworking Courses, Tutorials and Plans.

pirollo design

Design + build of contemporary furniture at Pirollo Design

Self-employment as a woodworker provides independence. It creates a unique situation where you can create wood products, furniture, or cabinets at a pace you are comfortable at, without anyone looking over your shoulder. You essentially become your own manager. If you are tired of the rapidly changing job market and the increasing demand for technology workers, woodworking can provide a degree of technical stability. The woodworking industry evolves very slowly. Unless you are involved in the highly computerized and automated CNC end of the market, the woodworking industry is very traditional.

There are many types of tools and machinery still in use today which date back to a century or more ago. This provides you with an idea of how relevant any knowledge you gain will continue to be useful in the future and not become obsolete. In my own business, I continue to use machinery and tools I purchased over twenty years ago. The techniques I use are the same as were taught to me thirty years ago. Compared to the hi-tech industry, my knowledge and skills would be obsolete by today's standards.

Creating tangible objects such as furniture, cabinets or wood crafts provides a true sense of satisfaction and enjoyment. You can measure your productivity through the work you create. Working at a woodworking business will motivate you to perfect your skills and techniques to produce higher quality work. Since businesses are inherently competitive in nature, you will develop processes and improve on current ones to increase your yield and improve your competitiveness. You will develop an appreciation for your woodworking business over time.

It can be overwhelming in the beginning, learning about the many aspects of running a business as well as seeking orders and commissions for your work. You will also need to weigh the advantages and disadvantages of becoming a self-employed woodworker compared to holding a day job. A day job often provides stability and a regular source of income without the need to worry about the next pay cheque. Of course, we know this is not always true especially in today's rapidly changing economy where the threat of downsizing or loss of a job is a reality. Until this occurs, however, the day job is a reliable source of income.

The disadvantages of spending forty hours a week at a day job is completely dependant on the type of work you do. Most importantly, do you enjoy what you are doing? If you are like many people in the workforce that gain little to no satisfaction from your work, you should investigate the idea of becoming a part time or full-time woodworker. In my own life, I have experienced downsizing and loss of employment on more than one occasion. This motivated me to develop a career I could rely on and become self-sufficient in the future.

Being in business for yourself involves much more than just woodworking. There are other aspects of a business you will need to take into consideration. Other aspects you will need to concern yourself with include accounting, inventory control, equipment and tool maintenance, purchasing, marketing, advertising, and shipping.

These aspects of a business take valuable time away from the core woodworking but are necessary for the business to survive and thrive. Today, there is an abundance of low-priced software to help manage a business and assist with accounting and bookkeeping. Software enables you to plug in numbers where the software performs all the background calculations for you. Over time, you will learn to manage these business-related tasks and revert to woodworking as your primary focus. I have not touched on the immense satisfaction derived from the independence and freedom of being a self-employed woodworker. Speaking from personal experience, I can attest that the freedom gained is unparalleled. It will no longer be necessary to dress up and commute back and forth to a workplace which provides little satisfaction but instead, mostly financial security.

Guaranteed jobs have also become a thing of the past. The often reduced and irregular income which is part of being a self-employed woodworker is well worth it in my opinion. You will need to determine if you can survive as a woodworker at this point in your life. This is accomplished by weighing your fixed monthly costs which include housing, family expenses, vehicle expenses, food, utilities, etc. Do you have a family dependant on your income or are you financially independent? Are you the sole income earner in your family?

If you are the sole income earner, it might be difficult and stressful to be able to survive monthly if your business income is spotty and does not meet your fixed monthly expenses. Instead, starting and developing a part-time woodworking business is perhaps a more viable solution. You will continue to draw on a regular employment salary while building your new business. Once you determine that the part-time business has grown to a point where you can survive from the income generated, you can give thought to leaving your salaried job. Many people opt out of careers at some point in their lives to pursue their passion. I have done this and not regretted it. As a former hi-tech employee, I derive significantly more satisfaction today in my woodworking business.

Self-employment is extremely rewarding! You will need to weigh the financial considerations of having to generate your own income vs. deriving an income from an employer in the decision of going into business for yourself. Many of these decisions apply to becoming self-employed regardless of the type of business. Woodworking is especially satisfying since you are pursuing your passion by creating tangible products where your output is measured in real, physical terms. One of the key qualities to becoming successful when striking out on your own is to have confidence in yourself. A high level of confidence will spur you on. Scepticism is your enemy. You need to minimize the level of fear and insecurity of starting your own woodworking business. Confidence will provide you the energy to offset the possibility of any setbacks experienced during the start up phase.

You might also experience doubt from the people that surround you, doubt as to whether you will succeed. Some people will go on about how difficult it is to succeed at your own business. These are most likely people that have never even attempted to strike out on their own. I too experienced doubt at the very beginning of my first woodworking business, during the business start up phase. I recall having more questions than answers at the time and every little step to self-employment was an adventure of its own. Within one year of starting and establishing my first woodworking business, I had absolutely no regrets of the decision. I told myself that I would have instead regretted not having started a business.

Tackling the many aspects of a business start up phase is a journey that everyone should attempt at some point in their lives. Early on, I convinced myself that I would invest one to two years in establishing a new woodworking business. At the very least, if it failed, a considerable amount of business experience would have been gained. The business did not fail, and I was instead encouraged to improve and grow the business and further define my product base.

Initially, mistakes in starting up a woodworking business are made, or should I say, errors are made that can be viewed as mistakes. These are often not mistakes; instead, they can be chalked up to naivety and a lack of experience. After all, how many people make the same mistake twice? I would recommend taking a general business course prior to beginning. This can be a workshop on starting a business at a community college or mentoring with existing business owners and learning from them. The business owners do not necessarily need to be woodworkers, but it would speed the process up if they are.

General business expertise is what you need and hopefully this book will begin the process and enlighten you to the many aspects of self-employment in the woodworking industry. If you do not currently have the skills to become a woodworker, you can study woodworking through a community college or woodworking school. Alternatively, you can apprentice with a knowledgeable woodworker, either as his assistant or in a mentor and student relationship. Many woodworkers are primarily self-taught and have progressed from basic woodworking skills to advanced woodworking skills simply by creating piece after piece and by reading and studying existing woodworking principles. The process of teaching yourself these skills and techniques can be lengthy as no one is available to correct your mistakes or provide you guidance, although this approach is entirely possible.

In my own woodworking career, I had struggled with some techniques, then followed a cabinetmaking program and returned to continue my woodworking. This progression resulted in better quality products and a much better understanding of woodworking. A few years later, I attended a fine furniture making school, the equivalent of following a master's program in woodworking. My woodworking skills increased dramatically after completion of a series of classes. The takeaway is that you should not be averse to following a formal education in woodworking.

The author, Norman Pirollo, at a woodworking bench in his furniture studio. Hand tools and machines are used to create the furniture in the studio. The author likes to call it a hybrid woodworking environment.

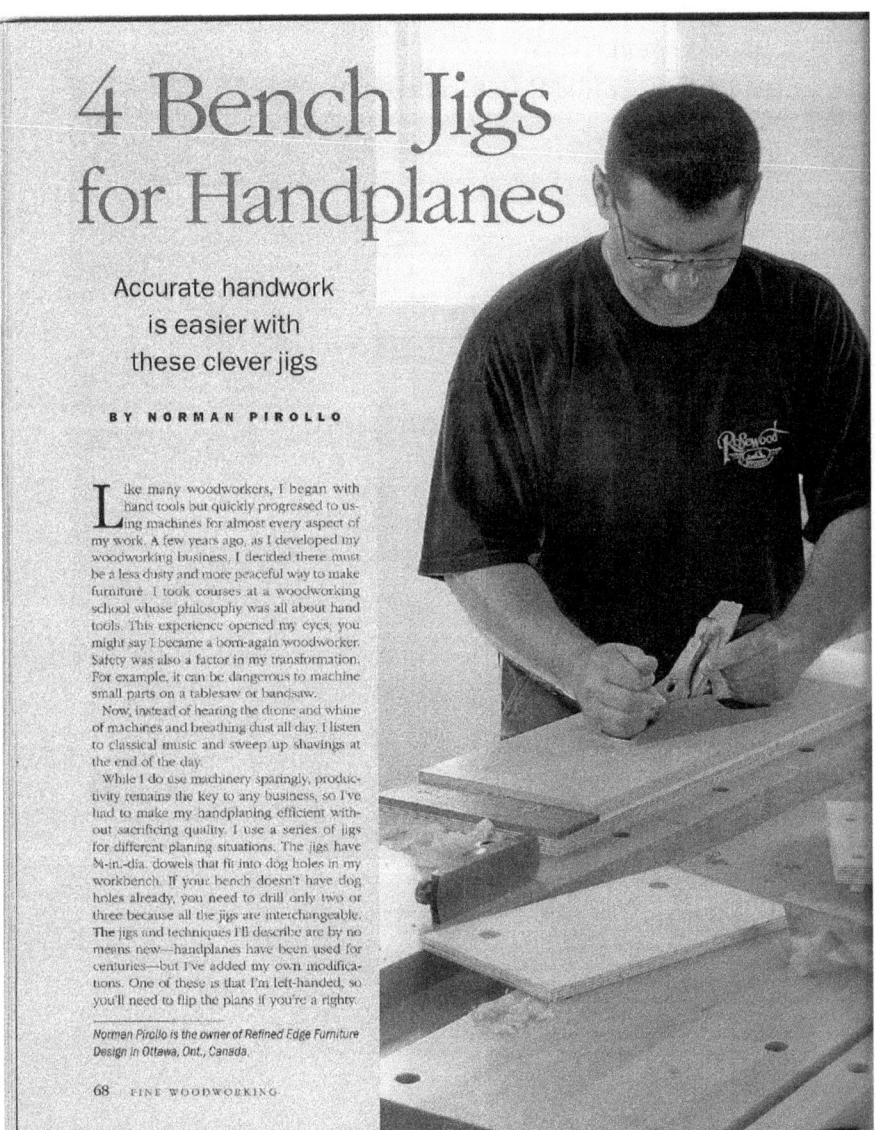

The author featured in a Fine Woodworking Magazine article on various bench jigs used in conjunction with hand tools. Courtesy Fine Woodworking Issue No. 202

Converting a Hobby into a Business?

You have probably been developing your woodworking knowledge and expertise over a long period of time. Most woodworkers begin woodworking as a hobby and slowly acquire the knowledge necessary to improve their skill sets. A woodworker can be largely self-taught or could have attended a woodworking school or woodworking institution. You will need to determine if your skills are at a level where you can confidently make wood products for sale. In many cases, a proficient skill level involves acquiring a formal woodworking education or a combination of woodworking education and being self-taught. Early on in my woodworking career, I attended a well-established college and followed a cabinetmaking program. Afterwards, I ventured out and put to practice the many skills I acquired.

A few years later, I decided to specialize in hand tool use and attended a smaller specialized furniture making school which focused primarily on hand tool use. In between, I created a thriving part-time woodworking business, **White Mountain Design.** Starting this business opened my eyes to the world of managing a woodworking business and juggling business responsibilities with my personal life. This small, thriving woodworking business was operated part-time while I kept my day job. During this period, the thought often crossed my mind of whether I should join the ranks of self-employed individuals.

Important questions to ask yourself

Have you made furniture, cabinets, or wood products before?
Are you comfortable in dealing with clients?
Are you familiar and proficient with joinery used in woodworking?
How skilled are you at applying finishes to wood products, furniture, and cabinets?

How long does it take you to make products or furniture?
Are you capable of working within deadlines?
Can you handle the marketing and bookkeeping that detracts from woodworking?

These and other questions are the core of any woodworking business, and you will need to cope with these issues at one time or another. Many people will mention that you should always keep your hobby as just that, a hobby. They will also say that once the hobby evolves into a business, the passion turns into stress and the enjoyment disappears. I am of a different opinion, however. Converting a woodworking hobby into a woodworking business has taught me to work within deadlines and to take on challenges I normally would have passed on. Being in a woodworking business has also enabled my level of work to attain new highs in quality. I attribute this completely to working with clients. A client, when not a friend or member of your family, has a greater expectation of quality. After all, they pay you for the wood product or furniture you create. The exchange of money for products raises the level of quality in the product or furniture you provide to your clients.

Another valuable trait developed in operating your own business is efficiency. I am not referring to efficiency in the strict sense of the word, where images of assembly lines appear. What I am referring to is the efficient use of valuable woods, the efficient use of valuable space in your shop, efficient use of time, and the efficient use of tools and equipment. These are all resources which can limit or further your success as a woodworker.

Two components of a piece of furniture or a product you create are:

1. The materials used in creating the wood product or furniture.
2. The time necessary to complete the wood product or furniture.

Maximizing material use reduces the cost of creating the furniture. Minimizing the time you spend creating wood products, furniture or cabinets allows you to create a greater volume of work within a defined time period. By maximizing your time and minimizing material use, you lower you input costs and can derive a larger net profit from your woodworking.

The efficient use of time is mentioned because as a hobby, there is often little to no pressure in woodworking. Deadlines are either not there or are extremely flexible. Maximizing profit is not part of the equation. A wood product or furniture is instead created as a passion or for personal reasons. This fact changes when you are woodworking as a business. Clients expect that furniture or cabinets will be ready on a certain date. You can easily factor delays into the equation, and this will provide you a buffer of time. The extra time allows for any unexpected problems.

Making more efficient use of time does not translate to creating an inferior product. On the contrary, by being more efficient you will have developed processes to be able to accomplish this. Along with processes, you will create jigs that aid in speeding up your workflow as well as creating more precision and repeatability in your work. When you can successfully interchange furniture components between furniture pieces is when your level of woodworking precision has attained excellency.

Expanding on Questions You Need To Ask Yourself

Have you successfully made furniture, cabinets, or wood products before?

This might come across as an obvious question, but the skills necessary for successful furniture and cabinet creation are a few steps beyond creating small wooden products. Knowledge of wood movement is particularly important, joinery skills are crucial, some design skills are necessary, and finishing expertise is almost essential today. Clients see the finish first, then the design, and then the actual construction techniques used to make the furniture and cabinets they might be interested in purchasing.

Dovetail joinery is a hallmark of quality to many clients. It is worthwhile to develop the skills necessary to create handmade dovetails.

Are you comfortable dealing with clients?

As in any business, client interaction skills are important. You need to be able to market yourself and your work on an ongoing basis. The client will ask why they should select you for their commission to build furniture or cabinets, instead of another woodworker. The client will need to be clear on the quality and style of furniture and cabinets you create. How do you differentiate yourself and your work from the competition or other woodworkers?

Most importantly, a discussion about the price of the furniture and cabinets will be necessary. Establishing a price is derived from sourcing the wood you will need, the hardware, the time spent in creating the commission, and your intended profit margin. It is best to clarify all this with the client before beginning. Ideally, you and the client should sign a contract outlining the specifications and details of the furniture or cabinet commission.

You will need to demonstrate confidence in any discussions with clients, as clients view this confidence positively and respect your opinion. As a woodworker, you need to be able to convince a client of your rationalization for a design and any design changes. After all, you have the design skills and understand the technical aspects of furniture and cabinet construction.

Are you familiar with the joinery used in making furniture and cabinets?

There are a large variety of joints which can be used in making furniture and cabinets. The tried-and-true ones are mortise and tenon joinery, dowel joinery, dovetail joinery and rabbet joinery. You need to become familiar with each type of joinery and when to use it. Some furniture components as in chairs are subject to greater stress and will need to incorporate strong, reinforced joinery.

Other components of furniture and cabinets are not as subject to high loads or stress and can be created with lighter, less rugged joinery. Decorative joinery is also a sign of quality with many clients, and the dovetail joint comes to mind. Clients often expect dovetail joinery to be used in attaching drawer fronts to drawer sides.

Another excellent reason to invest in strong, traditional joinery is to extend the longevity of the furniture or cabinet. Good joinery provides a strong mechanical connection for the wood components. Joinery can also be reinforced using splines and pins. If the glue in the joint ever fails, the mechanical component of the joint will compensate until the joint is re-glued. If there is a heavy reliance on a glue joint without reinforcement, the joint will likely fail before its time.

Another example of handcrafted interlocking dovetail joinery used in drawer construction. The series of drawers illustrates how repeatability can be used to your advantage. Here the parts are all cut and processed beforehand using a similar setup and process.

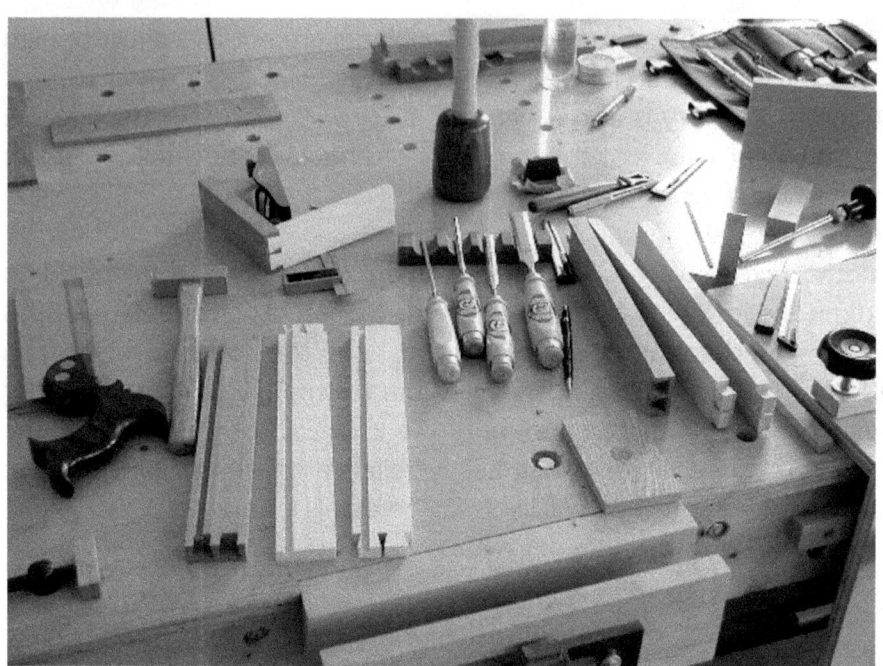

Drawer sides are being created above. Handmade dovetails are very often created with the shop-made dovetail jig shown below.

Different types of time-proven joinery which can be found in furniture and cabinet construction. Some of this joinery is designed to enhance the aesthetic of a furniture piece. Joinery can be hidden or prominent. More decorative joinery is designed to be strong but visually pleasing. Dovetail joinery and the joinery shown above are examples of this.

The mortise and tenon joint is one of the oldest and strongest types of joinery in existence. The mortise and tenon joint is an excellent example of a strong mechanical joint strengthened with application of glue. Mortise and tenon joinery is the mainstay of any furniture. It is wise to become intimately familiar with this type of joinery or the modern variant of loose tenon joinery.

An example of a three-way mitre joint with reinforcing splines. This shows the hidden mechanical connection of a woodworking joint.

How skilled are you at applying finishes to woodworking projects?

Furniture and cabinet finishes are as important as the actual construction of the piece. Clients like to run their hands over furniture and cabinet surfaces and feel the texture. Finishes can either be film finishes such as lacquer and shellac or finishes that have been absorbed into the wood such as oil finishes. It is necessary to discuss the finishing of furniture and cabinets with the client to avoid any ambiguity about the final product. Different finishes are used for different applications. As an example, since dining table surfaces need a much more durable surface than a hall table, polyurethane or lacquer are ideal finishes. Display cabinets can have a lighter shellac or oil finish applied, one which does not obscure the wood.

Finishes can be hand-applied or sprayed onto furniture or cabinets. A hand-applied finish is performed using brushes or lint-free cotton cloth. Hand application is a more traditional method of applying a finish to furniture. Spray finishes were developed to speed the finishing process in a factory environment. Small spray setups have since become available for the small shop. If you spray, a spray booth is necessary, one that is properly filtered and vented outside. I don't spray in my own workshop, instead I hand apply finishes. Most recently, I have begun using water-based finishes which have an extremely low VOC count and are environmentally friendly.

Wood finishing skills can be daunting and are usually learned over a period of time through some education and trial and error. Unless you have a formal woodworking education or have worked in a cabinet shop, it is likely you have not associated with knowledgeable wood finishers. You might consider taking a class or mentoring with a more knowledgeable wood finisher to learn proper wood finishing.

Sampling of the different type of finishes which can be applied by hand in a small shop environment.

An example of a high lustre shellac finish applied using a traditional French polishing method. Shellac mixing ingredients are shown below.

How long does it take you to make wood products, furniture, or cabinets?

The quick answer to this question is "**it depends**". The reason why the amount of time spent creating furniture or cabinetry is critical in a woodworking business is straightforward. You need to have good productivity to survive as a business. If it takes you months to make a single piece of furniture or cabinetry, you will create fewer pieces within a year and consequently derive little income from the business. Unless your furniture or wood objects command a very high price, it makes more business sense to produce a greater volume of products in a year. A woodworker in business that produces multiple pieces per month will do much better financially.

Initially, you will likely have very few commissions and very few orders; more time can be therefore spent on each piece. Until you begin receiving commission work and become busier and generate sales, the extra time will allow you to develop techniques and jigs to speed your processes up.

After a while, as your business grows and commissions and orders roll in, you will need to develop more efficient, quicker processes to create wood products, furniture, or cabinets. It is important to keep in mind that quality must never be sacrificed, even if this means reducing your workload and turning away work. I can attest to this principle as I have experienced this in my own business. To not sacrifice the quality of my work, I have had to turn away orders at one of my first businesses. Low quality work can be detrimental to any business, especially a woodworking or furniture making business. Negative word of mouth will quickly kill any future business. If you experience a client that is not happy or satisfied with your work, employ all means to correct the situation. It is best to deal with the client directly and resolve the dissatisfaction issue even if involves replacing the item or creating a new one. It is far too easy today for a client to spread their dissatisfaction over social media. This is to be avoided as news travels far and fast.

An example of a dovetail jig developed by the author to speed the process of creating dovetails. This dovetail jig aids in aligning the tail and pin boards to effect accurate marking. Chiselling out the tail and pin sockets are also performed using this dovetail jig.

Are you capable of working within deadlines?

When clients request commission work or place an order for furniture or cabinets, one criterion which often arises is "**when will it be completed**". Clients need to have an approximate completion date and you need to provide this. Unless you are a master woodworker with a remarkably high reputation where clients are lined up begging you to make them a piece of furniture or cabinets, the average client seeks a reasonable completion date. Clients have many reasons for requesting such a date, and they are often perfectly justified.

Once you provide a quote with a completion date, you need to work to have the furniture or cabinetry completed by this date. It is acceptable to insert a margin of a few days around the completion date, but not too many days. I usually quote a completion date and mention that the finishing process might take a few extra days depending on the time of year. In periods of high humidity, finishes tend to cure slower. Many clients place high value on your word.

A strategy is to provide the client with an outstanding piece of furniture or cabinetry, which in many instances is worth the wait. Delivering an order before the expected date will always yield beneficial praise from a client. On the other hand, if the delivery was unnecessarily delayed, the client will remember and take this into consideration when providing a word-of-mouth referral to other prospective clients. Remember, referrals and word of mouth are often your best, most effective marketing channels.

Can you handle business that detracts from woodworking?

You will soon realize that a woodworking business involves much more than woodworking. The allure of woodworking which originally drew you into starting the woodworking business also brings with it other aspects of running a business.

As mentioned earlier, the other components of a business are accounting, inventory control, equipment and tool maintenance, purchasing, marketing, advertising, and shipping. Exposure to these aspects of a business can be an eye opener. Before beginning my first woodworking business, I enrolled in a business education course at a local community college. This course enlightened me to the administrative aspects of operating a business. Many woodworkers handle this differently and engage a member of their immediate family or friends to deal with the non- woodworking aspects of the business.

For the rest of us, we fortunately or unfortunately need to deal with all the non-woodworking aspects of a business. It is best to simply embrace this and move forward. The best advice I can offer is to maintain good records which are quickly accessible, and to spend a few minutes each day administering the non-woodworking aspects of your business. Following this advice will spread the administrative load out over a period of days in the month. This helps to make the process bearable for the business averse crowd.

Of course, clients maintain a priority for your time. Any time spent conversing with clients is time well spent. Clients like to be updated as to the status of their commission although they will not usually insist on this. Regular updates to clients are highly appreciated in avoiding misunderstandings and ambiguities with the product they have ordered from you. Another option is to send out photos of the current state of the client's commission. Clients view this very favorably.

Part Time vs. Full Time?

The frequent evolution of a business is from a part-time to a full-time endeavor. Following this axiom is the safe and secure process by which most businesses succeed. It makes perfect sense to initially work at a woodworking business on a part-time basis while maintaining your employment.

The regular, stable income from employment provides a cushion to fall back on if your business fails or if the business idea is not viable. You can also determine if you have the mettle for business with this approach. If you fail after a certain timeframe, it makes no sense to convert your part-time business into a full-time undertaking.

Of course, there are reasons and scenarios of starting a woodworking business on a full-time basis that do make sense. For example, you have recently lost your employment; you have been downsized, cannot find employment, or have recently retired. These are valid reasons to take a leap of faith and start a woodworking business on a full-time basis. I need to add that to be able to accomplish this, you will need to have a sizeable nest egg of finances or have access to financing. This is to cover the start up costs of a woodworking business. Instead, starting a business on a part time basis enables you to slowly wean yourself off your day job while developing and building your woodworking business and clientele.

The financial security gained from maintaining your day job is invaluable since the risk factor of launching a business is minimized. This is exactly how I began my first woodworking business, on a part time basis. I juggled the demands of maintaining full time employment with the demands of developing a small business. Proceeding in this fashion enabled me to slowly ramp up the woodworking business and not completely rely on it as a sole source of income. I was also able to invest in equipment and tools early on as these are the cornerstones of a woodworking business.

Another advantage in starting a woodworking business on a part time basis is that you can take advantage of space within your home to operate the business. The space might be the basement, your garage, or an outbuilding on your property. Since the business is fairly small and being developed at this point, minimal space is typically necessary. Let's face it, you are not going to find or create a large clientele for your woodworking right away. Most clients are typically acquired through word of mouth.

Positive word of mouth is attained by selling to an initial base of clients or accepting commission work. Commission work can consist of furniture, cabinets, or wood products. Positive word of mouth is guaranteed by ensuring that a client is completely satisfied with their purchase or commission. Satisfied clients in turn, help you to find new clients and widen your customer base.

Using a portion of your property to conduct the part-time business, you will have saved considerably on one of the main expenditures of a woodworking business. Starting a woodworking business on a part time basis also enables you to take risks you would not normally take; this can be beneficial to the success of your business later on. As mentioned earlier, I began my business on a part time basis and spent a considerable amount of time in the evenings and weekends developing and perfecting the wood product I was marketing. You will soon realize if the wood product you produce is popular with clients.

Is it appealing?
Is it practical?
Is the price point reasonable?

A part time status also enables you to hone your skills and to develop techniques to create multiples or small batches. Multiples are the creation of more than one component of a piece of furniture or wood product with relative ease. You utilize this approach if you need to make more than one wood product that are similar to each other. Creating components in multiples will save you an incredible amount of time. This is often accomplished through the development and use of woodworking jigs. Jigs are the mainstay of a woodworking shop. Jigs also create repeatability in the components you create. Through use of jigs, repeatability is attained. Components are then dimensioned the same and with little tolerance. Joinery is also similar between components of a piece of furniture or cabinet. The advantage of repeatability is that you can easily interchange components between multiple furniture pieces. Jigs also allow you to create spare components for future projects.

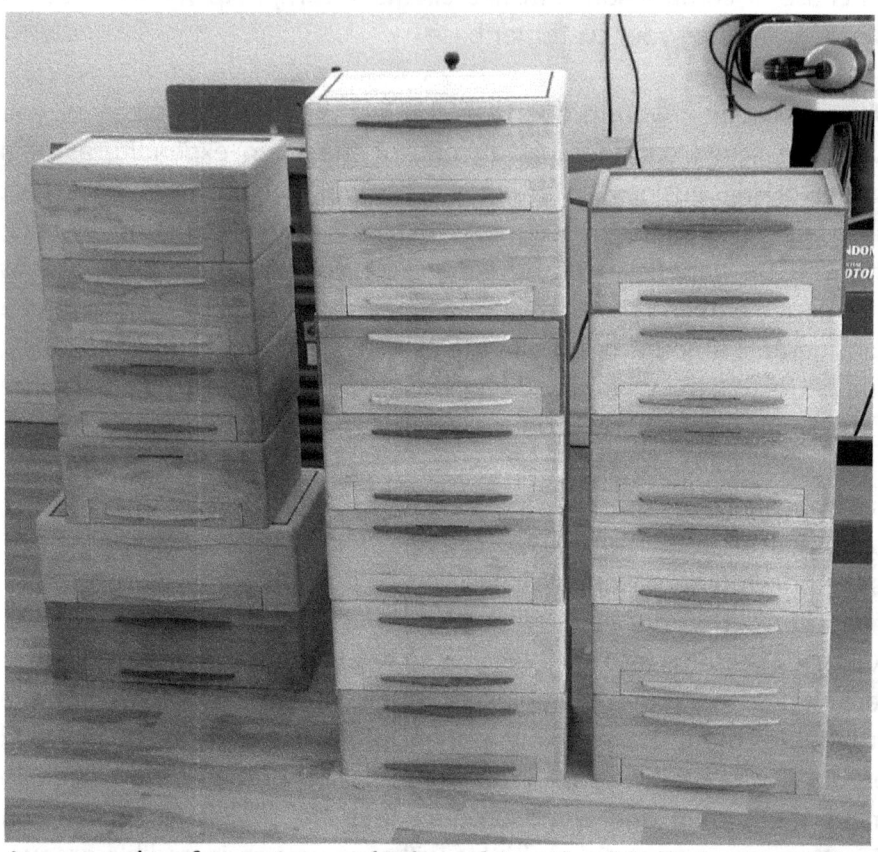

An example of creating multiples of jewelry boxes in the author's studio. The jewelry box components are created in batches while maintaining jig and equipment setups. Jigs are used to ensure all components are precisely cut and shaped. This saves considerable time and ensures that all components are identical in dimensions. Optional woods can also be seen on some of the jewelry boxes.

Another view of jewelry box multiples. The drawers are being created and will be fitted to the jewelry box cases next. The drawers are identical to one another and can be interchanged between the jewelry boxes if necessary. Some of the jewelry boxes have raised panel tops whereas others have flat panel tops fitted into grooves.

Another view of creating multiples of jewelry boxes in author's studio. Shown below, a completed mahogany jewelry chest with finish applied.

Finding or Creating a Niche for your Woodworking

There are many styles of furniture available in the furniture market and each of the styles appeals to a different clientele. Many people favour traditional furniture with period styling, whereas a large and growing segment of the population favours contemporary styled furniture. Style trends in the furniture marketplace can help you decide what type of furniture you should make for sale. Another consideration is the type or style of furniture you tend to enjoy making. If you favour a particular style of furniture and enjoy making this style, you will derive more satisfaction in the process. This will allow you to focus on the market segment that this style of furniture appeals to. As a woodworker, it is somewhat important to enjoy what you are doing, after all you have come this far and chosen a field you prefer rather than work at an unfulfilling day job. Why not go the extra length and choose to create furniture in a style which appeals to you? Using my own personal business experience as well as following careers of other woodworkers, I am confident that the market will be there for your wood product, furniture, or cabinetry.

Clients also sense that you genuinely enjoy creating work in a particular style and will purchase from you, or commission you to create the furniture or cabinetry they desire. Some facts are described in the following paragraph about period furniture and contemporary furniture. Period furniture, specifically styles dating from the 18th and 19th centuries, tends to be very ornate and includes carving in the design. I would say these styles are better suited to more experienced woodworkers. On the other hand, modern contemporary styles of furniture typically have straight lines and have next to no frills or ornamentation, simply basic design. This important fact makes contemporary styling more appealing to an enterprising woodworker. The amount of labour expended in creating contemporary furniture is considerably less than making period furniture.

Of course, you can completely bypass these existing styles and develop your own style of furniture. You can create your own furniture style and determine if there is a market for it. The furniture you design can be derived from existing styles. Many period styles throughout history are simply derived from earlier furniture styles. Your designs would then be considered designer furniture. Designer furniture does have a market, although the furniture would need to be created on a speculative basis. In other words, designer furniture and cabinetry are that which have been created and waiting for a buyer.

If you are currently making furniture that does not sell well or creating in a furniture style that caters to a small niche or client base, you might want to consider modifying it or re-designing it to have broader appeal. Small niches are fine, but this may limit the commissions you receive and the volume of furniture you sell. Appealing to a broader base, or larger niche, can be a good compromise. Your furniture style will be more appealing to a larger base of clients, resulting in more sales. Early on in my woodworking career, I began as a small box maker. The boxes were either straightforward, small single level jewelry boxes or small boxes with music mechanisms in them. Although sales were brisk, the price point of the boxes was low and not motivating me enough to continue pursuing this. While displaying my boxes at various small exhibitions, I began to ask clients who wandered into my booth what type of box they would like.

The feedback most often received was a demand for a large jewelry box, one with multiple levels and drawers. After listening to these people, I began to explore making larger jewelry boxes and humidors. I experimented with larger jewelry box designs and eventually designed a very appealing and well-executed jewelry box. This jewelry box style was appealing since it was the perfect compromise of interior compartments along with having an optimum size. This educational process was rewarding to me, and the result was well worth it. I then designed and built jigs to speed the process of making these new jewelry boxes, thereby increasing efficiency.

Considerable quantities of these large jewelry boxes or jewelry chests have been sold over the years. Seeking and appreciating client feedback can be applied to any product, especially handcrafted wood products. I find it to be one of the best forms of market research there is. A modern approach to seeking feedback is to conduct a survey of customers needs. Unlike having to reach out to clients directly as in the past, there is software available which can be adapted to your web site. This software can assist with managing a survey. Clients that visit your web site can indicate what product or variation of a product they prefer. The survey results can be beneficial to you in determining the direction to take with your products or furniture.

If you are unsure of what type of wood product to market, you can begin with simpler wood products. These are wood products that are straightforward to make, and you can then test the waters as far as sales are concerned. This will introduce you to the skill of marketing a wood product and acquiring clients. Once you have been successful with this approach, you can progress to more complex wood products or furniture and cabinetry that have greater appeal to you and utilize more of your woodworking skills.

You can also investigate the type of wood product other local woodworkers are making. This might provide you with a better idea of the market within your area. As an example, urban centers tend to favour more contemporary styled furniture, whereas non-urban centers favour traditional furniture styles or period furniture. Although this is a general statement and there is considerable overlap in the tastes of individual clients in either of these areas, this is a good guideline to follow. There are always novel ways to create a new product. Often, asking for client input of a product they would like to see is a good start. An iterative design process can come next to flesh out a new product. Creating a product to satisfy a demand is always a safe approach in any business.

An example of a contemporary styled hall table, designed by author, Norman Pirollo. This design incorporates metal and wood in a narrow profile. The hall table can also be configured as a shorter console table for a living room, showing versatility in the design.

Legal Considerations

As in any business, there are legal considerations to understand and grasp. Product liability is a concern as you are essentially creating a product. Liability for furniture that falls over or falls apart and possibly injures someone is a primary concern. For this reason, when I design my furniture, I take stability into consideration. Furniture placed against a wall needs to have a greater depth to decrease the likelihood that it will topple over. An example of this would be a freestanding hall table. Tall bookcases, regardless of their depth, will likely need to be attached or bracketed to a wall. Other liability concerns are injuries acquired from wood products, perhaps very sharp corners need to be eliminated on chairs or furniture that are lower in height.

You will need to check with your insurance company and be up front with them as to your intentions for either a part-time or full-time woodworking business. They can guide you to what amount of liability insurance coverage you will need and inform you of which wood products they do not cover for insurance purposes. For example, many insurance companies do not cover the manufacture of baby furniture due to the high risk of injury and subsequent liability. When I began as a part time woodworker, I had an optional rider added to my home insurance for a woodworking business located in part of my home. Since the business was not my main source of income and annual income derived from the business was low, the home-based business rider was very reasonably priced. Insurance companies will often determine how large a business is from the annual income derived from it. A few years later, I expanded to a larger full-time woodworking business. At this time, the insurance company directed me to purchase a commercial insurance policy which is separate from my home insurance policy. My current two-level workshop on my property is attached to the home and is fairly large at 1300 sq. ft. Due to this adjacent workshop; it is obvious my insurance company wishes to minimize their exposure to liability and damage claims.

The commercial insurance policy has a larger liability portion which covers the issue of clients visiting my workshop, an overarching concern of insurance companies. The insurance company will ask pointed questions about the size and scope of your woodworking business and base the insurance premium on annual sales, size of the workshop, and exposure to liability.

If your woodworking business is conducted in a part of your home, another consideration will be zoning, noise, and any signage you might wish to put up. It is best to verify with your municipality if it is acceptable to have a home-based woodworking business within your area of the city. Chances are it will be fine if there is no loud noise emanating from your garage or through open windows in your home workshop area. Signage can be an issue, however. Speaking from personal experience, most municipalities frown on business signs placed on urban or suburban properties. In rural areas, however, this is more acceptable, especially on main rural roads. Zoning regulations typically accept home-based businesses, as this is quite common today.

Often, it is best to quietly maintain a woodworking business so as not to raise the ire of neighbours. If the business has relatively few clients visiting, the impact on the street you are located will be minimal and it will not be obvious that you are running a business. The reason I mention this is that many municipalities frown on businesses that have a large clientele coming and going.

The business structure of your woodworking business is also a consideration. You can set up a business as a sole proprietorship, a partnership, or a corporation. In many cases, a small business begins as a sole proprietorship. This business classification is the least expensive and simplest to create and administer. The other classifications, partnership, or incorporation are optional. Although it involves a considerable amount of paperwork and cost, incorporation can be beneficial to you in the long run.

The advantage of a corporation is that it completely separates your business from your personal assets, greatly limiting any liability you might be exposed to. There are also tax advantages of setting your business up as a corporation through reduced tax rates if income derived from the business is kept within the corporation. As an example, if you draw any money from the corporation as a salary, this amount is then taxed at regular income tax rates. Also, be aware that there is an additional cost incurred on a yearly basis for administering an incorporated business.

Setting up your business as a sole proprietorship provides you the ease of entering the world of self-employment without too many headaches. You can either choose your own personal name for your business or select an available name of your choice. Administration involves keeping and maintaining paperwork of all your business-related expenses. This includes paperwork for all income derived from the business and the fixed and variable overhead costs along with advertising costs.

If your business is viable and you wish to continue or possibly expand, you can in the future create an umbrella corporation that includes the sole proprietor business you have already created. It is always wise to consult with an accountant on how to properly structure your new woodworking business. Getting it set up correctly at the beginning will save you much grief afterward. My own businesses have been set up as sole proprietorships. I decided on this approach to save myself the time and expense of having to complete corporate tax forms.

If you have set your business up as a limited corporation, there will be separate accounting to maintain for the umbrella corporation as well as for any of the individual businesses within the umbrella corporation. It is prudent to weigh the pros and cons of each business setup and then go from there. If the business is very small, sole proprietorship makes sense. If you are launching a large business with one or more employees, incorporation is more viable.

A Business Plan

You have probably heard the term "**business plan**". This is little more than a roadmap for your business. A business plan maps the direction a business should follow over a period of years. Business plans are written with certain criteria in mind. A business plan defines your market and niche, defines what product or products to focus on, and defines the progression in the size of your business.

I must admit I was not a big fan of business plans early on and just waved the whole exercise off. My first business took off and I was more concerned with developing and improving products. The market found me, and the volume of business received was sufficient if not overwhelming at times. I also deviated from my original business focus as I discovered new opportunities.

It was only a few years later, after attending a business school and following a formal education in business that I began to appreciate the importance of a business plan. Business plans keep a business focused and keep the business from deviating in directions which do not grow the business. Initially, the business plan is developed through considerable market research. You either enter an existing market for your product or you are developing a new market for your product.

The clientele of a business enjoys purchasing from a business that demonstrates knowledge and expertise in a particular market or niche. By deviating and pursuing other short-term paths, the credibility of a business can be damaged. The client becomes aware of this deviation from your business marketing, and instead seeks out another, more focused business. Your local bank and business experts will almost always recommend that you develop and write a business plan before starting your business. You should follow this advice as it forces you to invest serious thought into the direction your business should follow.

Perhaps you have already had success with a particular product and wish to create a business around that product. This is entirely acceptable and demonstrates that you will be successful at developing a business. Your market is already in place and clients are seeking you out. However, it is always best to develop a business plan with more than one product in mind. If the demand for a single product drops off, demand for a second or third product can compensate in the downturn. A business offering more than one product will also be able to tap into a greater and more diversified market. A business plan will help you think this through. A bank or investor in your business will look positively upon the business if it offers more than one product. In the end, the success of a business is all about mitigating risk.

With the fixed and variable costs associated with running a business, it becomes important to maintain a steady flow of orders or commissions. There are other costs such as maintaining an inventory of lumber and hardware components to be able to produce the products you are marketing. It makes more economic sense to purchase large quantities of components to receive volume discounts. If you do this and sales for a product, drop off or disappear, you have an inventory of wood and hardware components that you no longer need. Repeating this for a few products can become expensive and you will set your business up for recurring losses. Purchasing large quantities of specific material and hardware should only be performed for products that are guaranteed to sell or for those which you already have outstanding orders for.

A large part of a business plan is also to develop a marketing plan. Marketing the product or products you intend to manufacture is key to your business' success. Having said this, marketing involves a plan and an advertising budget. Advertising costs can rapidly increase in a short time. It becomes important to determine which advertising works and which does not.

What Equipment and Tools Do I Need?

You can build wood products, furniture and cabinets with both machinery and power tools, or strictly with hand tools. Most production-oriented woodworking shops will use machinery to maximize efficiency and speed production of wood products. Smaller woodworking outfits instead use a hybrid assortment of machines and hand tools in their shops. The machines are primarily used to prepare and process lumber for the fabrication of wood products. Smaller power tools and hand tools are used to create joinery and used in later stages for finishing and detail work.

As a small woodworking business, you would want to invest in some machinery. The machinery can be used to pre-process lumber to where it can be dimensioned for use in woodworking. The machinery I refer to are a jointer, planer, and bandsaw or table saw. I highly recommend a bandsaw, as it is one of the most versatile pieces of equipment in a woodworking shop. With today's emphasis on reducing dust and working in woodworking environments with minimal dust; efficient dust control has become a necessity. All powered machinery and smaller power tools generate some form of dust, either fine airborne dust or larger particulates such as wood chips.

Dust control should be installed at the source and the preferred method is to capture dust before it becomes airborne. Dust control takes the form of central dust collectors or cyclonic dust collectors. There is piping or tubing located at each piece of machinery leading back to the central dust collector. Alternatively, or optionally, an air cleaner should be installed in the shop to remove airborne dust. This airborne dust is what you breathe. Since this fine dust is exceptionally light, it will float for a considerable time in a shop environment. The air cleaner cycles shop air through it and within minutes will scrub the shop environment of fine airborne dust.

Some of the recommended equipment for a woodworking shop will be as follows:

Jointer (6 in. to 8 in. wide)
Planer (13 in. to 15 in. wide)
Bandsaw (14 in. to 17 in. throat)
Tablesaw (2HP or 3HP model)
Drill Press (16 in. floor-mounted)
Router Table (2HP to 3HP plunge type)

The list above reflects machinery installed in a typical woodworking shop. There is also another aspect to woodworking that involves using hand tools, either exclusively or together with machinery. Hand tools often provide greater control of the woodworking process. Machines are great when efficiency and repeatability are important, whereas hand tools provide another dimension to the process. Use of hand tools enables you to exercise more flexibility and control in creating certain features of your wood product. The use of hand tools also creates a quiet and peaceful shop environment.

With hand tools, there is next to no dust generated, instead small chips and shavings are created. Hand tools in a woodworking shop also create a balance. In fact, many shops have separate machine rooms (to process rough wood) and bench rooms reserved exclusively for hand tools. When it comes to hand tools, I believe it is better to invest in higher quality hand tools rather than low priced alternatives. High-quality tools will likely last your lifetime, are much easier to adjust, and offer consistent results. Several high-quality hand planes and chisels used in my own woodworking shop have been purchased over a twenty-year period. Over the years, my style of work has evolved where today I fully embrace the use of hand tools in a woodworking shop. I have devised methods of work to increase efficiency when using hand tools. Hand tools definitely have their place in most small woodworking shops today.

Shown is a 15-inch thickness planer. This model can handle most board widths available and has a 3HP motor on a 220V circuit. I use this thickness planer primarily to prepare wider boards. The bandsaw on the next page is the mainstay of my shop, used for every project I work on. The bandsaw is a Delta 14 in. model that I have owned for over 20 years. It is modified for improved dust collection through two large dust ports. It has also been upgraded for resaw capability.

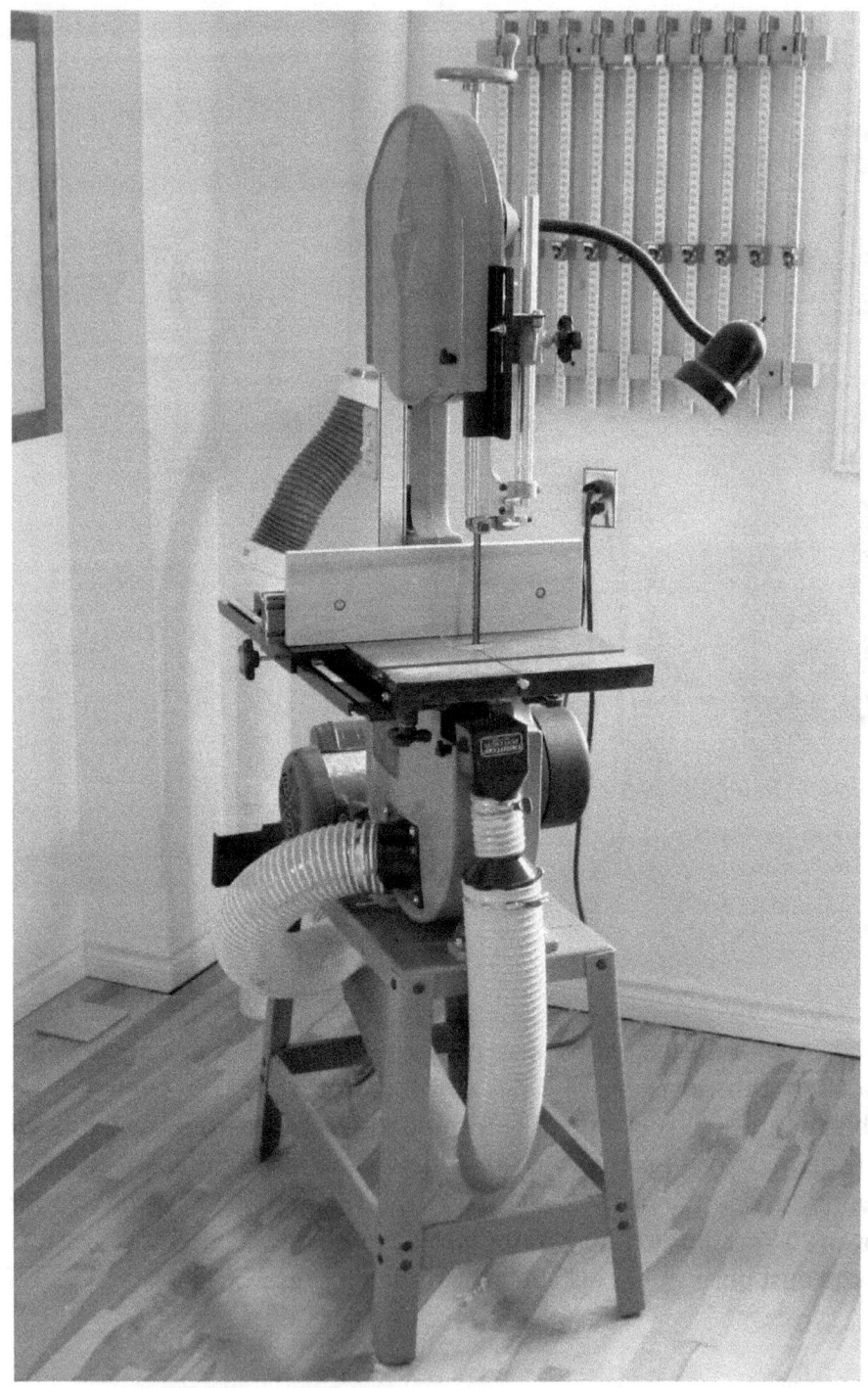

A small list of hand tools to consider for woodworking and furniture making as follows:

Set of Chisels (to create mortises and dovetails)
Hand Planes (for preparing and finishing surfaces)
Squares (for precision and accuracy)
Workbench (with a front and tail vise)
Dovetail saw (to create dovetail joinery)
Rip saw (for ripping wood)
Back saw (for crosscutting)
Shooting Board (for precise end cuts)

The use of hand tools will initially result in a much slower process than using machinery. You will find that after a certain amount of time, the efficiency gained from using hand tools will begin to offset the productivity gains of machinery. Let us not forget that machinery needs regular maintenance and setup, and this time needs to be factored into the overall time required to build furniture and cabinets. I tend to favour a hybrid shop environment where both machinery and hand tools are used together.

There are instances, however, where woodworkers work exclusively with hand tools. Often, the reason for this approach is the fact that they cannot run noisy or dusty machinery in their locations. Another reason is that they have developed a woodworking philosophy of working exclusively with hand tools. Another likely reason is that they prefer the hand tool process and the accompanying peacefulness and quiet that goes along with it. For example, you can live in a condominium and make small wood products in a spare room. It is entirely possible to accomplish this using hand tools and a solid, proper woodworking bench.

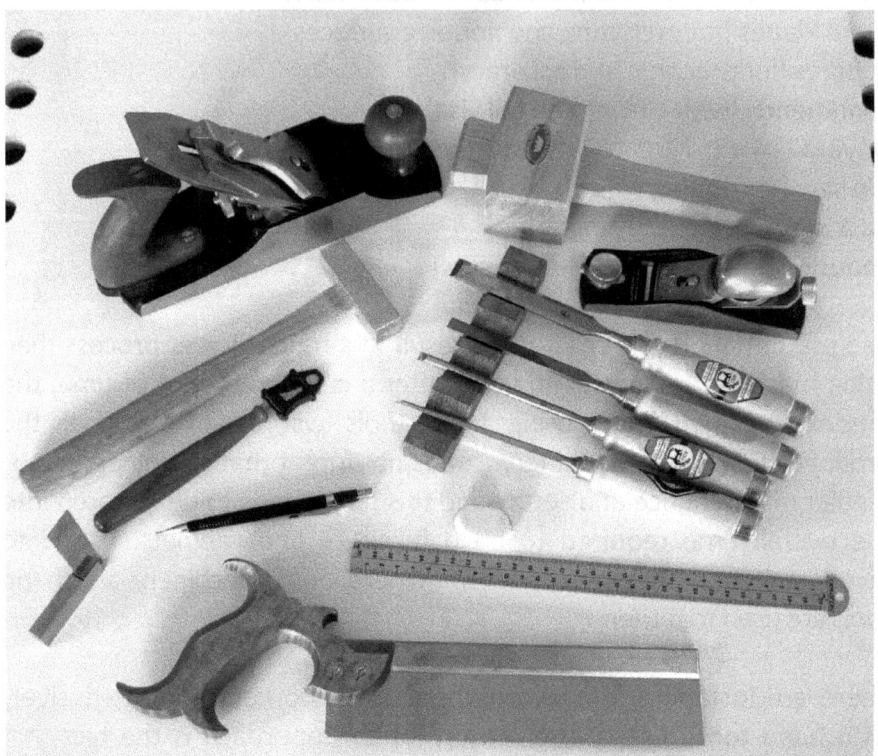

An assortment of typical hand tools used in a workshop includes measuring and layout tools as well as tools used to create joinery such as dovetails. Shown are a set of bevel-edge chisels, commonly used hand planes, a fine backsaw and marking and measuring tools. My advice is to invest in higher quality hand tools, they are more precisely built and simpler to adjust. The metal is also a superior grade which minimizes the possibility of distortion. It is easier to attain a higher level of precision with better quality hand tools.

One of my hand plane racks. An assortment of handcrafted and restored hand planes is shown. The wooden hand planes have been crafted in my woodworking studio. To the left are a series of hand planes I manufactured through White Mountain Toolworks. An antique transitional plane can be seen at the far end; it has been restored with a new sole. The metal fore plane in the center is a modern, high quality No. 6 hand plane offered by Veritas Manufacturing. Second from right is a very long No. 7 high-quality jointer plane offered by Lie-Nielsen Tools.

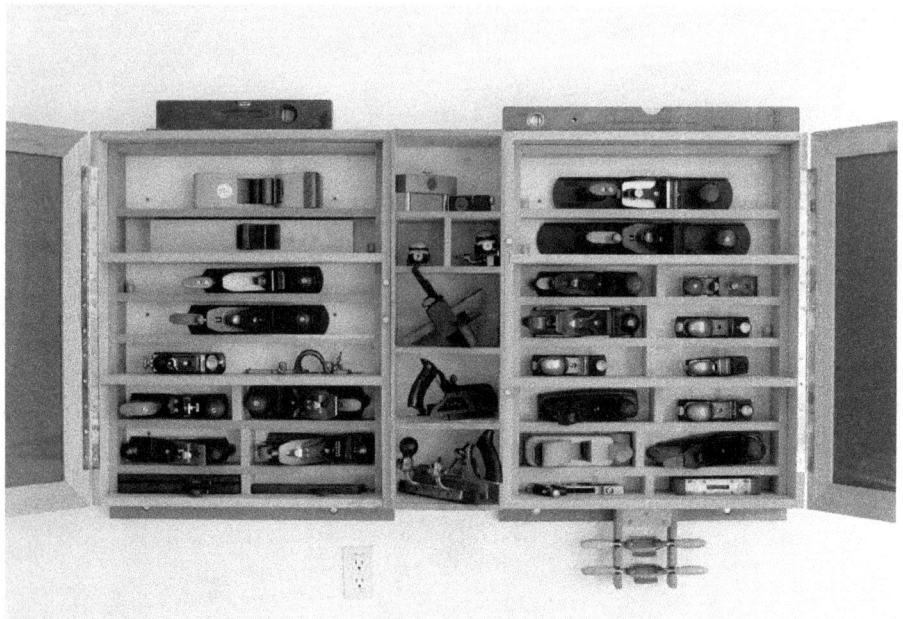

Another of the hand plane cabinets in my workshop. Enclosed cabinets keep hand planes free of dust and offer a dry environment. Keeping moisture away from tool steel will prevent any oxidation or formation of surface rust. Dust also attracts moisture. It is wise to keep tool steel free of dust whenever possible.

The hand tool approach greatly minimizes noise and dust, and you will be able to work at any time of the day or evening without disturbing your family or neighbours. If you decide on using hand tools as a component of your woodworking, you will need to become familiar with sharpening processes and techniques. Hand tools require regular sharpening to be effective.

A blunt chisel can be a dangerous tool since greater force is necessary to slice through wood; extra force which can lead to injury. I always maintain my hand tools, especially chisels and hand plane blades, to a high degree of sharpness. You will find that having very sharp tools will make the extra effort of using them in your woodworking safer and more pleasant.

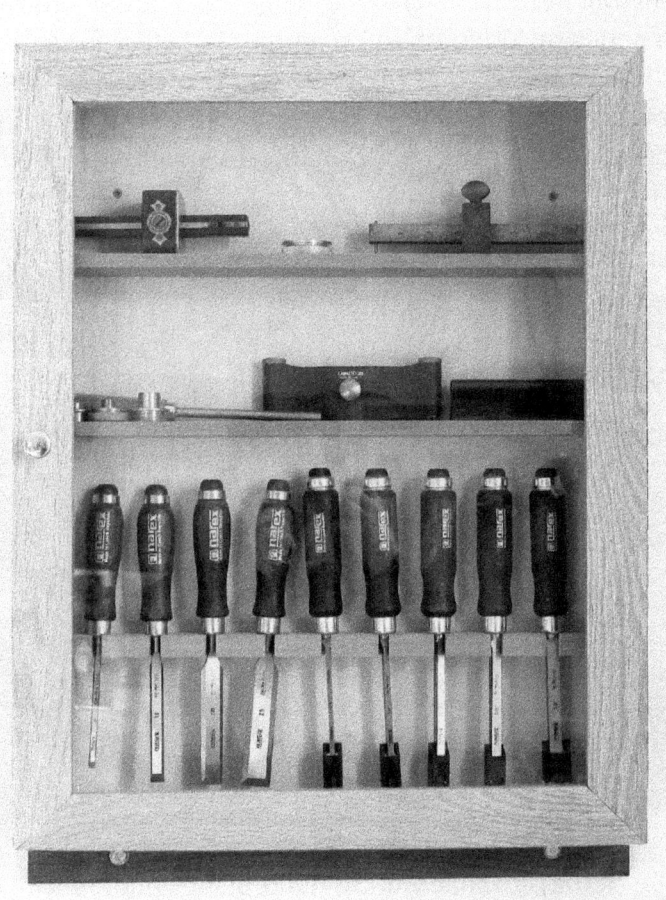

Another enclosed tool cabinet with two types of chisel sets and assortment of layout tools. Rather than glass, the door panel is made of a safer Lexan. Glass can easily shatter and has no place in a woodworking shop.

After a few years you will tend to develop best practices to work in your woodworking business. These practices will instill efficiency and quality into your furniture, cabinets, or products. You will also tend to develop and make different jigs used to create repeatability of furniture components. If for example, you need to make a large series of similar chairs, it would make sense to develop jigs to speed the creation of the necessary components. Jigs also ensure that each component will fit multiple chairs exactly. Jigs are also reusable if you develop a series of furniture you plan on marketing for several years. Precision is ensured through use of woodworking jigs. I use a fair number of jigs in my own woodworking. Often, the jig is used for a unique operation, where other jigs are more versatile.

Small parts are being shaped using hand planes and bench jigs in the author's workshop. This bench jig fits into the round dog holes of the workbench. These bench jigs were developed several years ago to aid in work-holding of small components on a workbench surface.

Fitting display cabinet doors in the author's workshop. The cabinet case is created first; the doors are created afterwards and slightly trimmed to size using a combination of block planes and bench planes. When fitting parts together, very small shavings can be removed through use of hand planes and chisels.

How Much Space Do I need?

The space requirements necessary for a woodworking shop vary. Some woodworkers work on an individual wood product at a time, whereas others work primarily with hand tools and minimal use of machinery. With an emphasis on hand tools, space requirements can be in the order of 200 square feet or so. If you build larger products, furniture and cabinets and utilize an assortment of machinery, the space requirement of a shop increases considerably.

A machinery-intensive shop environment needs a minimum of 500 to 600 sq. ft. of space. It is necessary for each piece of machinery to have sufficient space surrounding it to both safely operate the machine and maneuver boards successfully within its radius. Often, in many shop environments, the machine area and bench areas are separate. The noise and dust associated with machines is therefore isolated from the bench area of a woodworking shop. This is usually accomplished by installing either a swinging door, or at the very least, heavy plastic strips hung vertically and overlapping each other. The best method is to enclose the bench room in its own enclosed room or space.

Another aspect of a woodworking shop is the assembly area. This is the area where wood products are dry fitted, assembled, and later glued together. A space within the shop also needs to be reserved for applying finish to the wood products and this space needs to be relatively dust free.

Lumber will need to be stored in another area of the shop, preferably stickered (each board separate from the other) or laid vertically against a wall in bins. Lumber can either be laid flat or vertical. If vertical, the lumber is more accessible, and it will be easier to pull individual boards out. It is important to let the wood breathe and acclimatize to the shop area, therefore plenty of open space surrounding the wood is necessary.

Other considerations for a woodworking shop are higher than normal ceilings to be able to swing longer planks around without hitting light fixtures. In my own workshop, I had nine-foot ceilings installed. Plenty of ambient light and artificial light is recommended for your workshop. In my shop, I have banks of dual fluorescent fixtures. These banks can be switched separately depending on the amount of light necessary at a particular time of day or evening. An investment was also made in several large windows to bring in as much ambient light, as necessary. The large windows cut down on the need for artificial light. When light is necessary for a bench operation or while using a particular machine, it is wise to set up task lighting to provide additional lighting at the machine. This also eliminates the requirement to turn on the main shop lights of the workshop. The overhead shop lamps are connected in two separate banks in my own woodworking shop.

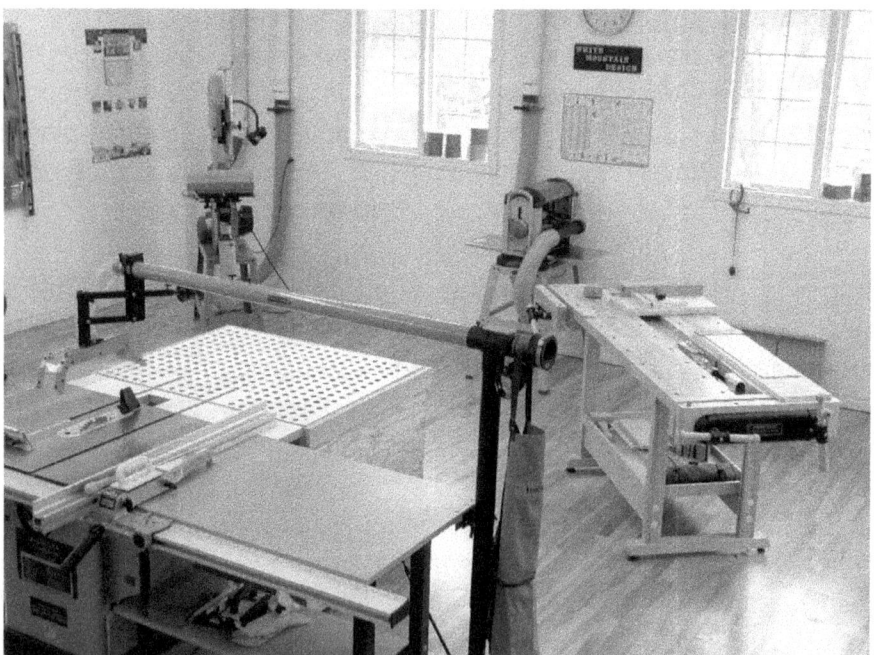

An overhead view of the bench area of my workshop. This is part of the upper level of the workshop. The workshop is designed for maximum use of ambient light. It is also well lit through banks of overhead lights.

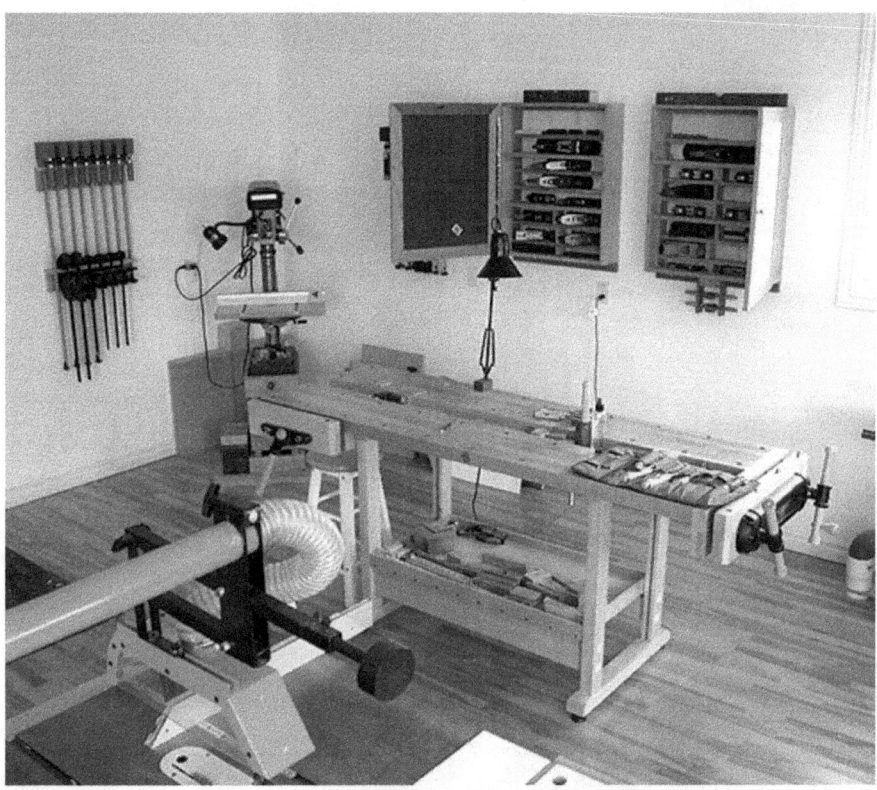

Another area of the upper level of author's workshop in this view. This is a second workbench area with wall-mounted cabinets containing a selection of hand planes. Narrow profile machinery is placed in the corners of the workshop. Plenty of space is provided around the workbench to create a more effective, safer environment.

Developing a Product or Products

Probably the most important aspect of a woodworking business will be what type of wood product to produce. The type of wood product or furniture you intend to create can be based on an existing style or a completely new style. Before jumping in and simply making wood products, it is critical to perform market research within your general area (region, city, state) or the area you wish to market your wood products. You will need to weigh the result of this market research against the type of wood products you enjoy making.

The ideal situation is to find a match in your local market for your intended furniture or wood product. In a perfect world, you create furniture or wood products you enjoy making, and hopefully find a good market for it. However, this is often not the case. Popular furniture styles are often produced by other area woodworkers and there could possibly be competition to your business. This should be taken into consideration when pricing your work. If you have local competition, a variation of a popular style can be a (**USP**) or unique selling proposition of your work.

Other selling points can involve the techniques you utilize in creating your wood product or furniture; perhaps you tend to use hand tools exclusively. Certain clientele value the handcrafted aspect of wood product creation, while other segments of the population are simply interested in the end product regardless of the means used to create it. In my work, I combine unique design with a large component of handcrafting. My work, therefore, appeals to a broader range of clients interested in these features. I have also decided to create contemporary, modern styled furniture which appeals to my own taste. This decision somewhat limits the market I can sell into, but it allows me to specialize within this specific style or niche. In making this decision to create a style of furniture which is appealing to me, the motivation and inspiration to create this furniture is maintained.

Part of the product development process is to gain feedback and critique of your work. The most valuable feedback is from your clients or prospective clients. If the clients tend to favour a particular wood product or style of furniture you create, it is in your best interest to explore this further. Sometimes this is a product you are not fond of making, and perhaps modifying it slightly makes it a more interesting build. A slight modification in the design will not detract from sales and in many cases, makes the product more appealing. Often, a woodworker stumbles on to a popular style of product or furniture and then adds specific detail to the wood product to distinguish it from a competitor's product.

The type of wood product or furniture you create will be a personal decision. You need to determine if you prefer to make multiple, identical wood products or instead follow a unique, **one-of-a-kind** woodworking path. The one-of-a-kind path is where each furniture piece or wood product is inherently different from a previous design. Both paths have advantages and disadvantages. The advantage of unique, one-of-a-kind wood products or furniture is that it appeals to a certain clientele; the ones who will pay a premium knowing they have a unique piece of furniture. This allows you to make fewer pieces and set a higher price for each piece of furniture or wood product.

The disadvantage to this approach is that unless you have a commission from a client to design and make a specific wood product or piece of furniture, it will be necessary to create products or furniture on a speculative basis. Speculative work (**on spec**) is work that is seeking a buyer or client. This process can get expensive as you need to front the material and hardware costs along with the time involved. High quality wood and hardware used to make furniture or wood products can be expensive. There is also the risk that the wood product or furniture you create does not sell and instead occupies valuable space in your shop.

A series of hand plane models developed by the author for White Mountain Toolworks. These hand planes are entirely handcrafted in wood and address a niche in the woodworking market for wooden hand planes. The irons are provided by Hock Tools.

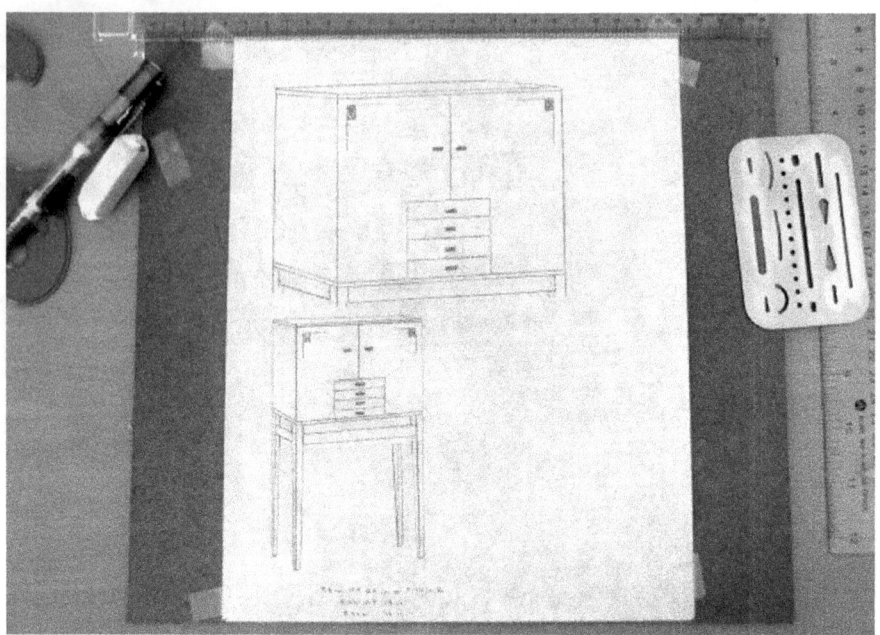

Preliminary conceptual drawings for a one-of-a-kind showcase cabinet for a client. Two versions of the display cabinet are shown.

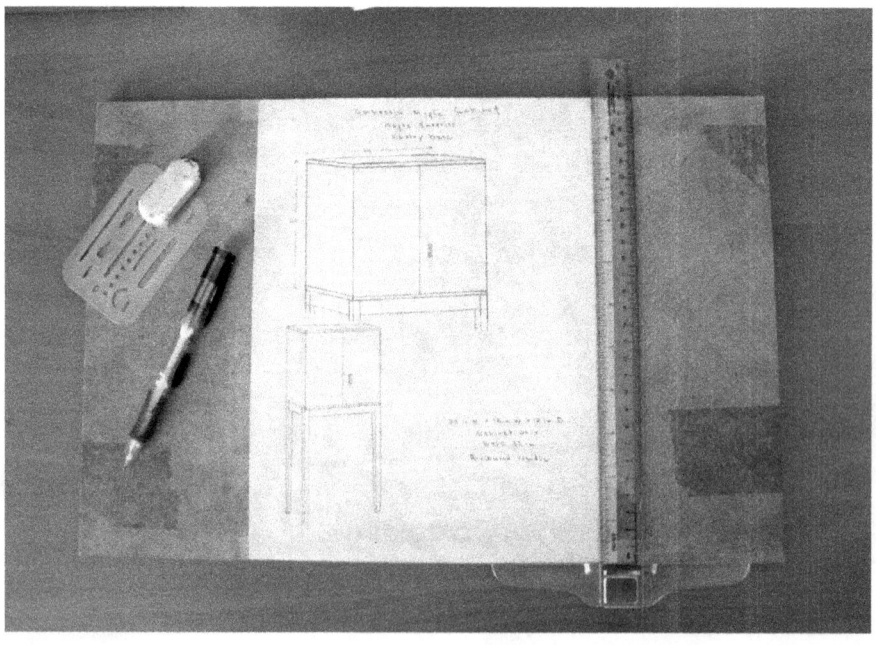

Alternatively, you can decide to make multiples of a wood product derived from a pre-existing design, and this may be in your best interest. The multiples will eventually sell as you have most likely selected a popular design or style. Following this formula, your inventory never grows to an unreasonable level and the risk level associated with creating speculative, uniquely designed wood products is eliminated.

The design process is a structured process. A sketch of a wood product or furniture is the initial step. This stage then progresses to preliminary drawings and then to a series of measured drawings. The measured drawings contain specifications for the dimensions of the furniture or wood product as well as describing the hardware to be used in the furniture or wood product.

I typically use **CAD** (Computer Aided Design) software for more complex projects such as standalone cabinets and chairs. The use of CAD greatly speeds up the design and rendering process. Using CAD, I can modify the dimensions of a design and view it within minutes as opposed to re-drawing it on paper. CAD enables you to view the project in 3-D so a sense of scale is more apparent. The furniture can also be visualized in 3-D and rotated to view the sides and back of furniture. CAD is slowly replacing sketching and drawing as a preferred method of design. Conceptualizing the furniture on a screen in 3-D is extremely advantageous in the design process. Rendering of furniture is easily accomplished afterwards. The furniture can also be viewed in a room setting using CAD and other widely available software. It is well worth the investment to learn to use CAD in your own woodworking.

The natural progression of the design cycle is to then create a scale model or maquette of the design. The maquette (**scale model**) has scaled down dimensions of the proposed furniture or wood product. The maquette can be used to present a design to the client for consideration and for their opinion.

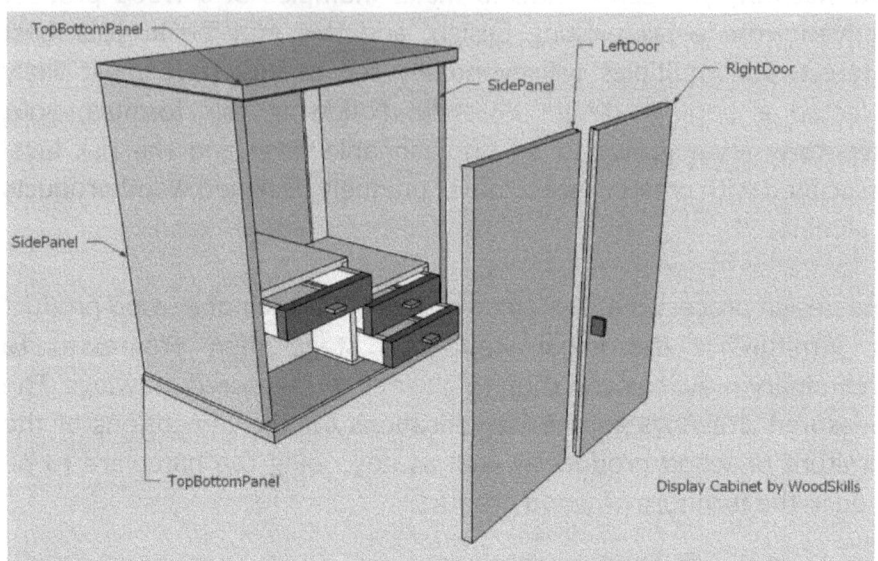

CAD rendering of a standalone display cabinet. The components of the cabinet frame, drawers and door panels are shown. The components of the interior and drawers are shown below.

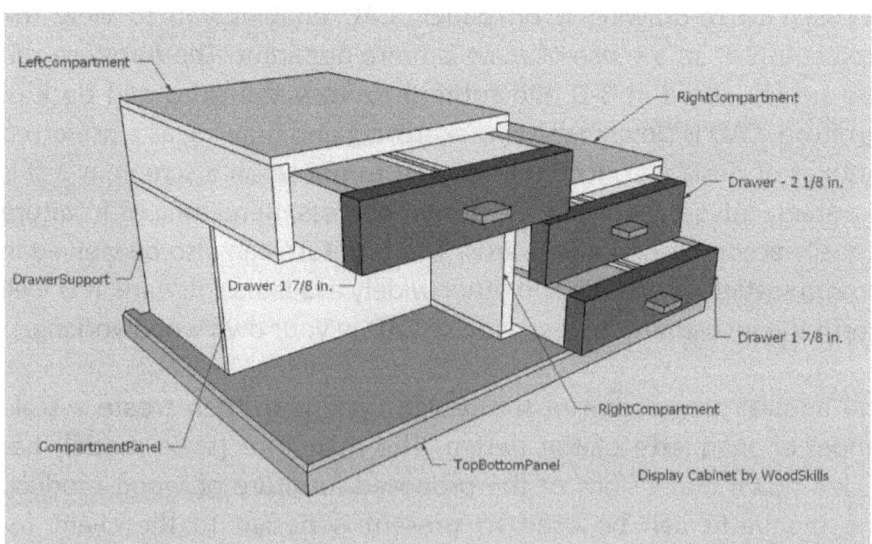

CAD rendering of the interior compartments of the standalone cabinet shown earlier.

Occasionally, after creating a scale model or maquette of a design, a woodworker realizes the design is flawed, not structurally sound or not visually appealing. With a scale model of a design, these criteria can easily be determined and visualized. Rendering a design in 3-D using CAD software has become the modern-day equivalent of using maquettes or scale models. Design changes can then easily be made. It is much preferred to apply changes at this stage of a design rather than create a poorly designed or unappealing piece of furniture or product. Components of the wood product or furniture design can also be mocked up in full size for a much better idea of how they fit into the overall design.

A small maquette or model of the base for a hall table with curved legs.

An example of mocking up doors for a display cabinet using white cardboard. The outlines of the door frames are also drawn on the cardboard for a better indication of the visual appeal and layout. Modifications can easily be made using this approach.

A maquette or scale model of a hi-back lounge chair, used to determine the viability of the design. The individual components are cut from hardboard and hot glued together. Outlines for openings in the chair legs can also be seen.

Creating or Finding a Market for Your Work

Just as important as developing the right mix of wood products or furniture to market is the research into finding a market for your existing wood product. There are two aspects to this. The market already exists for a popular furniture style or the market for your work does not exist. If a market for your furniture or work does not exist, you can then create a market for the unique, higher quality furniture in a style you enjoy creating. In this case, it will be necessary to find the clientele that appreciates your furniture and finds it appealing.

Today, with the prevalence of ubiquitous mass-marketed furniture and wood products which lack quality; a premium is placed on quality handcrafted wood products and furniture. The handcrafting process provides a client with a much greater selection of woods, natural finishes instead of heavy opaque stains with a muddy look, and quality joinery designed to last generations.

The attributes of fine, handcrafted wood products are a (**USP**) unique selling proposition and should be used extensively in your marketing. Marketing your work can be performed either on a small budget or a larger budget with formal advertising. You can begin by spreading the word that you have begun creating wood products or furniture for sale. The word-of-mouth approach is effective, although it is much slower than taking out a large ad in a local newspaper or local magazine.

One of the best marketing tools is a satisfied client. A client who has either purchased your wood product or commissioned you to create a wood product or furniture can become a considerable marketing tool. A satisfied client can leverage other sales for you by simply spreading the word to their friends and colleagues that you do excellent work. With the advent of the Internet, it has become increasingly important to have a web site to provide prospective clients with information about you and your work.

I cannot overstate the importance of this as most if not all your competitors will have web sites. You will therefore be at a disadvantage if not using the web as a marketing tool. Today, the web site has essentially replaced the "Yellow Pages", but in a more enhanced form. I have had web sites for my woodworking businesses since 1998 and they have been invaluable in getting orders. Formal advertising can be expensive. You need to be selective about the most successful medium to advertise your woodworking business and focus on this particular medium. Advertising department representatives will tell you that you need to run ads consistently over a few issues to gain acceptance with the readership. There is some truth to this although this approach can be an expensive undertaking.

Most publications offer discount rates if you place an ad over a few issues; this is something to consider. The type of magazines to advertise in will be local home style and decor magazines; ones that appeal to clients who are in the process of or will soon be furnishing their homes. Most magazines will provide the ad set up for free if you plan to become a regular advertiser, or if you lock in for a few issues. My advice would be to begin with a small ad and determine the feedback you receive from this ad. The ad could initially be a text ad that can be later upgraded to an ad with an image or business logo. Larger ads are more likely to attract clients in a shorter time. The return on investment of larger ads will most likely be of benefit to you.

Creating a market for your wood products or furniture can be accomplished through clever marketing if you build unique wood products or furniture not based on existing styles. Marketing for a unique type of wood product or unique furniture need not be advertisements. It can instead be a story in a local newspaper or magazine profiling you as a woodworker, with photos of your work. This can be accomplished by having a satisfied client contact the newspaper or magazine or contacting them yourself. Newspapers and magazines place value if you are doing something unique and different in your woodworking business. The story then becomes newsworthy!

Examples of a unique product, technique or process are the use of an ecological source for your woods, or the re-purposing of existing furniture, or recycling wood, which was destined for a landfill, etc.

Another avenue to market your wood product or furniture is through a craft gallery or local store which accepts work from artisans on a consignment basis. This is an excellent means of getting the word out that you make wood products or furniture. These galleries and consignment shops typically ask for 40-50% of the sale price as their commission. Although this commission appears high, it can be well justified. The exposure you will receive from having work in their gallery or consignment shop is simply not available to you through other means. I have followed this path numerous times and had success with it. An added benefit to this approach is that certain clients will seek you out for specific commission work after having seen the quality of your work in a craft gallery, furniture gallery or consignment shop.

An ad for Refined Edge Design in an "interior design" trade magazine.

An example of a few labelled promotional items created for an interior design show for Pirollo Design, formerly Refined Edge Design. The investment in promotional items can often be justified at trade shows. The items will attract people to your booth where you can establish a dialog with them about your work. Discussing your business and work with clients is invaluable in bringing an awareness to your wood products or furniture. Prospective clients will tend to remember these conversations and act on them in the future.

Creating a Portfolio of Your Work

One of the best marketing tools is the portfolio. A **portfolio** is a chronicle (photo series) of the body of work (wood products or furniture) you have created over time. Usually, your best work is part of the portfolio as it highlights the type of work you can make. This portfolio is then presented to your prospective client. The client usually wishes to see examples of your work to determine if your skills are up to par, if your sense of design is good, and to see a variety of your work. The portfolio consists of high-quality photographs of your work. In the case of a print portfolio, the photos are larger than usual and of higher resolution. A good portfolio can serve to sway or convince a client that your woodworking expertise is exceptional, and you have successfully completed commissions.

You can also include photographs of the wood product or furniture you have created in home settings (**in situ**), to provide the client with a better idea of how your style of wood products or furniture can fit into a home. Print portfolio binders used for your photographs can be purchased at office supply stores. The quality of the photography in a portfolio is critical and the photographs should be taken by a professional photographer. If you have photography skills, the necessary lighting and a DSLR camera, you can accomplish this on your own. The furniture or wood product is typically placed on a light-coloured backdrop to create a focused setting for the furniture and to not detract from the furniture itself.

In addition to a print or hardcopy portfolio, you can create an online portfolio that also presents a sampling of your work to interested or prospective clients. The photographs need to be correctly lit and of high resolution, although the resolution is not as critical with web-based photography as it is with a printed portfolio. The resolution for photos in web-based photography does not need to be as high because monitors cannot display a high resolution beyond a certain point.

An online portfolio displayed either through an online gallery or through your own web site is available to a broader audience and is available every minute of every day throughout the year. Online portfolios can be quickly and simply updated and modified. You can easily add new furniture pieces or wood products, modify pricing, change product descriptions, etc.

The print or hardcopy portfolio is a marketing tool for you to carry around when meeting with prospective clients. It also provides the client with ideas for a custom piece of furniture of their own. You should also include sketches and drawings of previous furniture you have created in the print version of the portfolio. The sketches are to help the client visualize how the design of a furniture piece begins with a simple sketch, progresses to a set of drawings and ultimately to the actual creation of the furniture.

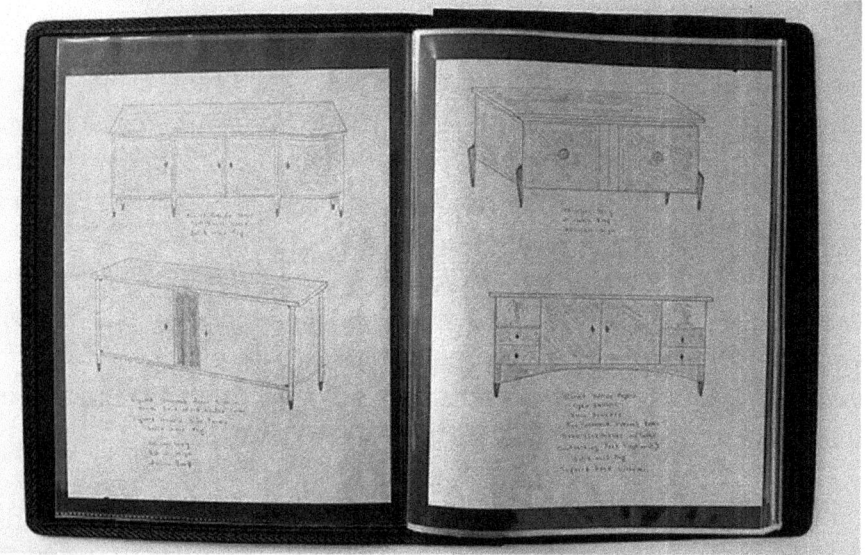

A series of drawings and dimensions of a credenza shown to a client, after consultation of the necessary criteria. Multiple design variations in different styles were prepared for this client. A few of the variations can be seen above.

Examples of commissioned furniture in a print portfolio of furniture, supplied by the author. Actual hi-res photographs of completed furniture pieces as seen in one of my print portfolios.

Internet Marketing

Only a few years ago, advertising and marketing was largely performed through traditional mediums such as magazine ads, newspaper ads, and of course, the ubiquitous yellow pages. Today, with the advent of the Internet and the many online resources available to you, it makes complete sense to have an Internet presence for the woodworking business you create. This Internet presence will likely be in the form of a web site. This web site can offer a gallery of your furniture or woodwork product and include a section devoted to your biography, work philosophy or style of furniture. Also necessary is information about how to contact you, as well as purchasing and commissioning information for interested or prospective clients.

In my case, a web presence has been available since 1996 through existing gallery web sites. A first woodworking and furniture related web site was developed for my business in late 1997. Web sites of this era were somewhat primitive as web site software at the time was new and had not been perfected or standardized. Digital photography was in its infancy in this period, although it greatly simplified the process of photographing wood product and furniture pieces and make the images available online. Today, web site software quality and variety has increased dramatically, costs have come down, and there are plenty of skilled individuals available to create your own web site. I have witnessed this evolution over a twenty-year period and can gladly say that it is much more pleasant to create, update, and market web sites today. Web sites work hand in hand with social media in making the public aware of your business and furniture or products.

Digital photography technology has also progressed exponentially over this period, and costs have come down considerably. Web site hosting fees are very reasonable today. All this makes it much more appealing and affordable to have a web site today. Another factor to consider is that your competition will likely already have a web presence, so it becomes necessary to publish and have your own web site hosted simply to remain competitive.

Web site developers can be easily found in most cities, and you should shop for both the best price and quality of web site you will have designed for you. I need to add that the ongoing maintenance costs of hosting and updating a web site need to be factored in as well as the initial cost of creating and publishing a web site. You can, alternatively, design and create your own web site. Today, several web site companies exist that will host your web site as well as enabling you to create the web site yourself. Templates are typically used to perform this, but the results are good. I have used such a process at one point and was impressed at the quality and ease of creating the web site.

Photographing the wood products or furniture you create also becomes an important criterion at some point. Some furniture makers shoot their own photography, whereas others hire professional photographers to drop in once a month or so and photograph their work. If you decide to perform your own photography, you will need to invest in all manner of photographic equipment. Vital equipment includes a tripod, a large backdrop; auxiliary lighting and preferably a high quality DSLR type camera. Most importantly, you will need to take workshops to learn how to perform studio photography.

Today, I combine my own photography with that of professional photographers at my own web site. If a piece of furniture can not be easily photographed, I will not hesitate to contact a professional photographer for the task. It is well worth it in my opinion since my time is valuable and outstanding photography can make a commission or sale. The takeaway from this is to not always take the most inexpensive path in your marketing. Better quality marketing often leads to sales which more than compensate for the extra cost of the marketing tool, be it photography or advertising.

Coping With the Ups and Downs of a Business

Most businesses experience ups and downs, usually related to business cycles, or having something to do with the state of the economy. The period of 2008-2011 was dismal for many home furnishing and decor businesses. This can be completely attributed to the state of the economy and the ongoing recession. During periods such as this, people tend to spend much less on furniture and home decor, and instead keep the wood products and furniture they already have while waiting for better times. The experts will maintain that this is a great time to consolidate a business, trim the fat and eliminate the non-profitable aspects of the business. This makes complete sense since there is not much else going on with the business regarding sales.

The down phase of a business cycle can often wreak havoc with a business. Woodworkers who have not already experienced a down period can be in for a nasty surprise as to how quickly business drops off. It is prudent to not overextend yourself financially in your woodworking business as inevitably the down portion of a business cycle will occur. Of course, all this business cycle knowledge is gained with experience. If you are a relative newcomer to the business world, you will likely not have experienced a downturn. The most recent recession was unusually long and placed many woodworkers in hardship as the upturn in the business cycle took a few years to occur. The takeaway is to be prepared for this eventuality and to not extend yourself and your business too far financially.

Another option in keeping a shop humming during a slow business period is to design new wood products and furniture or to work on interesting variations of existing wood products or furniture. You can also update your skills by attending focused training of new woodworking techniques or learn a completely new skill to incorporate into your business.

This type of education is often available at private woodworking schools or even local community colleges. An excellent reason for updating skills during a business downturn is that when business improves there will be no time available to update your skills. You will never know how long the window of sales opportunities will last during an upturn in business. It is best to take complete advantage of this upside in the business cycle. When business is good there is also no time to make changes in your business. You will likely be producing wood products or furniture at a steady rate and cannot afford the downtime.

Very often, during periods where I either have no commission work or have recently completed a piece of furniture for a client, I take time to inspect my equipment, machinery and sharpen hand tools and blades. I find it important to correctly maintain equipment as it increases the reliability and longevity of the equipment. Good working equipment is also less likely to break down during a critical phase of a furniture build. Maintaining equipment also keeps me busy in the shop. It is during these slow periods that I have sufficient time to perform these tasks. Business cycles are unpredictable, as well there is no certainty that you will ever experience a downturn in business. It is however, prudent to be prepared of the eventuality of a downturn.

Maintaining Balance between Business and Personal Life

Sometimes we can get carried away with a business and spend more time at it than perhaps we should. I am as guilty of this as anyone. I find that when I spend too many consecutive hours in my shop that I begin to rush my work and become impatient. My furniture making is performed on a full-time basis now and I follow guidelines about how much time to spend in the shop on a daily basis. I keep the maximum time at seven hours per day or close to this. Often, I will spend an extra hour in my wood studio in the evening if applying a finish to a piece, to allow it to dry overnight.

This guideline of time spent in the shop was determined through many years of experience within a shop environment and by following other full-time woodworker's experiences. Very often, after too many hours in the shop, it becomes increasingly difficult to maintain focus especially if performing repetitive work. This becomes a safety concern, and it is usually when accidents occur. Too much time spent in the workshop can also impact your personal life. It is prudent to maintain a balance between work and life. It is often difficult to force yourself to stay away from your passion, but often it is necessary to simply walk away and maintain a good work-life balance in the process. Your spouse and family will appreciate this and are more likely to support you in your business endeavor. This is from personal experience.

Family and friends will greatly appreciate this and support your business to a larger degree if they notice it does not overwhelm you. Early on, when beginning my first part time woodworking business, I worked at my business in the evenings and weekends. For the sake of maintaining a good work-life balance, I would only work in my shop a maximum of three hours per evening. Often, I worked less and made sure to allocate time to my family.

I find it too easy to get carried away and lose track of time when in the workshop. Following a guideline of maximum shop time is an excellent starting point in maintaining a good work-life balance. As in every field, time spent outside the shop is often just as important for your business as time spent within the shop creating wood products or furniture. There are numerous tasks necessary to run a business such as accounting, inventory, purchasing, contacting clients and bookkeeping. In my own business and personal life, a considerable amount of time is invested in reading up on current furniture trends and new woodworking techniques.

As well, improving on existing woodworking techniques will enable you to create better and more marketable furniture. Time spent **"outside the shop"** attending woodworking conferences and shows is also essential in interfacing with other woodworkers. This step helps the owner of a woodworking business become aware of new trends and explore new business opportunities.

Often, simply establishing a dialogue with other woodworking business owners will make you aware of an improved approach to running your business. Other woodworking business owners in your area or region can become your allies where business opportunities can be shared. Some woodworking businesses sub-contract work to other businesses that specialize in creating certain components. They have the in-house expertise to perform the task well. Often, if a woodworking business is overwhelmed with work, it can be advantageous to refer a client to another woodworking business. The other business will likely reciprocate one day.

Maintaining the Passion and Motivation

Over the years, I have managed to maintain my passion for woodworking despite several ups and downs experienced. The business cycles referred to earlier can sometimes discourage a woodworker from continuing on. There is always an upturn in business after a downturn or bottoming of a business cycle. The good times in business are always guaranteed to return!

Occasionally, if a woodworker continually makes the same wood products, interest may begin to wane. In times like this, I enjoy designing a new product or develop a variation of an existing furniture design. This re-creates interest in making the piece while growing and expanding the market for the furniture design. Designing new furniture or wood objects will also serve to challenge you. In my own business, I often seek challenges. It is appreciated when a client asks for a certain element or feature in a piece of furniture. This causes me to go research on how to do it. I consider this an addition to my skill set to possibly use in a future commission.

Of course, if you are making period furniture styles that typically have minimal styling changes and follow the original design, this plan will not work. You can instead design a completely new piece of furniture in the period style you are accustomed to. Afterwards, you can determine its acceptance in the market. I spend a good amount of time learning new techniques to incorporate into my furniture designs.

Often, woodworking techniques are gained through the design of a commissioned piece of furniture. I find that it is essential to regularly challenge myself and take on new techniques or processes. As an example, early on in my woodworking career I had some difficulty with finishing processes where the finish on a piece of my woodwork or furniture was simply not satisfactory or marginal at best. Discouraging as it was, I persevered and read up on finishing techniques and asked many questions.

I experimented and tried different approaches to applying finish. Today, I can confidently say I am extremely satisfied with my finishing process and make it a selling feature of my work. There is a saying that mistakes often lead to opportunities. Often, correcting a mistake will open your eyes to a new technique or feature.

Woodworkers tend to isolate themselves in their shop for extended periods of time and then occasionally surface. Woodworking can be an intensive process since so much is occurring simultaneously. Often, much joinery needs to come together quickly and accurately. This can demand complete focus for extended periods of time. It is easy to get carried away and focus on the work at hand while neglecting other aspects of a woodworking career.

The importance of the social aspect of woodworking cannot be overstated. Meeting with other woodworkers either formally through associations or as colleagues is critical to rekindling the flames of inspiration. Joining a woodworking group or association will allow you to share your successes with your peers. Other woodworkers in the group can also provide advice and guidance, especially if they are in business. Most woodworking groups typically hold monthly meetings with a specific theme or topic. Guest speakers are often invited to speak on this topic. Members of the group also speak on their experiences and expertise. I have spoken on several occasions at the woodworking association I belong to. This created an opportunity for me to share my knowledge, make people aware of what I do and learn more about the subject I am presenting.

Inspiration is often what drives a woodworker to create new designs, to explore new aspects of woodworking and to modify existing designs to be new and exciting. Attending woodworking conferences also inspires a woodworker to push the boundaries and create a new style of work. Whenever I attend woodworking shows and symposiums, I am made aware of what other woodworkers are working on and how perhaps I might be interesting in pursuing a similar path. Networking with other woodworkers should be a focal part of your business.

Creating Excellent Client Relationships

Clients are the very heart of a woodworking business. We need to listen to their opinions, value their critique, and attempt to please them through their commission or purchase.

Earlier, I referred to marketing strategies where the client can bring you a valuable element of marketing. This is feedback from the client. Granted, not every client appreciates all the work you perform in creating their furniture or cabinetry. Since they have invested in you through your woodwork, they bring to you a marketing opportunity which is word of mouth advertising. I cannot stress how critical it is that that each client feels that they have received the absolute best product you create.

Maintaining this high-quality approach for your clients and their respective commissions automatically provides advertising in the form of word of mouth. This is inexpensive advertising that you do good work. Another facet of a woodworker and client relationship is the handcrafted aspect of the wood product or furniture you create. Many people place greater value and cachet on handcrafted work and not so much on furniture or objects that originate from a factory. The sweat equity and skills invested in creating high quality wood products and furniture cannot be compared to cookie-cutter wood products and furniture originating from an assembly line.

Each handcrafted wood product or furniture piece is slightly different from the other in a subtle way; emphasizing the fact that assembly line processes were not used. Some anecdotal prose follows. Early on when I was a beginner woodworker, I did not have the confidence that I was creating my best work. At the time, I had been working on different processes to improve the quality of my woodworking and had not yet perfected any of these processes.

I decided to move ahead and market my woodwork regardless, since the feedback received from immediate family and colleagues was sufficiently positive in encouraging me to continue. Sales were not spectacular; they were dismal. Although several clients were satisfied with their purchases, I felt in my heart that the quality of my woodwork needed to improve considerably. It was also during this period of reflection that another woodworker at a small, local exhibition I was selling my work at wandered over to my booth. He gave me some of the best advice ever. He pointed out what I was doing right and what I should not be doing.

This advice was taken to heart, and I returned to the drawing board. His advice echoed similar feedback being received from people looking at my work. Prospective clients often do not feel it is their place to provide a critique of a woodworker's work, especially if they are not experienced in the field. The woodworker that provided me the advice, however, was a valued contributor to my later success as a woodworker. This lesson is one that I have never forgotten.

The moral of the story is to keep an open mind and try to acquire independent feedback about your work. Sometimes showing your work to a more experienced woodworker can be valuable to the path you have chosen. It is best to find out early on if your furniture or product needs improvement. Does either the construction of the furniture or product or design need to be improved upon? Only independent critique will provide you with the answer. Client feedback is a good starting point.

Making Furniture and Wood Products on Commission

Expanding on the client maker relationship, a major source of a woodworker's business can be in the form of commissions. Commissions can be best described as an agreement between the woodworker and the client to create a custom piece of furniture or wood product. The custom piece of woodwork originates with a design, either supplied by the woodworker or supplied by the client. Alternatively, the design can be custom, unique, and provided by the woodworker in collaboration with the client.

The collaboration between client and maker is effectively a joint design process where the client provides the idea or rough sketch of what they would like. The woodworker then refines this idea into a tangible design. The woodworker needs to consider several criteria into the refinement of the design. Criteria include the correct proportions of the furniture or wood product, the stability of the design, and the skill level necessary to create all components of the furniture or wood product. Availability of special exotic woods and necessary hardware is also important in the initial design.

All these factors must be considered before finalizing any agreement to build the furniture or cabinet for a client. Another good reason to work out the design and details is it helps considerably in arriving at an accurate cost and price estimate for the commission. It is easy to under price work and not completely factor in the additional labour necessary for either complex joinery or detail work.

The type and availability of wood used in constructing the furniture or wood product also needs to be factored in and completely costed prior to proceeding with a commission. A small percentage of extra wood is always necessary, in the order of 10-15% of any wood product or furniture construction.

This is typically waste wood and very often neglected in the pricing. The labour component of making wood products and furniture will need to be correctly estimated when pricing a piece furniture or custom order. It is easy to underestimate the time (hours) necessary in creating a custom piece of furniture or wood product. The estimate needs to include finishing time as well as the time spent designing and building.

Finishing the wood product or furniture can consume a considerable amount of time, especially if the finish is hand-applied with multiple coats and then polished. Once you have created a few pieces of furniture on commission, you will become better at accurately estimating the cost of building a single piece of furniture. Another consideration is the time spent sourcing the woods used in constructing the commissioned furniture or wood product. If common domestic woods are used, they can likely be sourced locally. If highly figured woods, either domestic or exotic are necessary in the design, these can be much more difficult to source from local wood distributors or retailers. The highly figured or exotic woods will likely need to be ordered from outside your local area or region.

If the design of the furniture or wood product of the commission is one of your existing designs, the estimating process will be much simpler. You should always maintain detailed records of every component of a particular piece of wood product or furniture you create, and the time associated with making it. This step will help considerably in arriving at an estimate of a new commission for a client.

Occasionally, you will need to construct special jigs to be able to form or shape certain components of a commissioned piece of furniture or wood product. The time spent in designing and creating these jigs should be at least partially factored into the final estimate for the commission. It is important to determine if the specialized jig you have created will be used again for other furniture you make. In this case, consider absorbing a portion of the time spent making the jig and only bill the client for a portion of the time. Most of the furniture I create is commission work and unique in design.

The design process I use typically involves a few meetings with the client. The design process ensures that the design is correct and is acceptable to both the client and I, therefore removing the possibility of any misunderstanding later. The client is also provided with detailed drawings of the piece of furniture being created for them, so they are clear on what I am making. This approach avoids any surprises later. When providing the detailed drawings, I ensure that the client does not approach another furniture maker with the design. The design belongs to the woodworking business. This is important information to share and for you to remember in your own client meetings.

Good surprises about the commission are different, however. Occasionally, I will add a small detail to enhance the beauty of the furniture, and this pleasantly surprises the client. I find it especially important to accurately price my work to not feel that I am being taken advantage of. When my work is priced correctly, there is greater satisfaction in creating the furniture. I also then place extra focus on any detail work.

An example above of a large, commissioned wall art for a client. This wall art piece is 6 feet wide and 2.5 feet high and is composed of three veneered panels of figured woods with highly polished metal components. This was the first of a series of wall art pieces created in my furniture studio.

Diversifying and Expanding

There will come a time in your business when the following thought crosses your mind. Should I continue with the business as is or expand it? This completely depends on what your expectations are of the business. Keeping a business small makes everything more manageable. The downside is that any income derived from the business will be capped due to your output limitations. A larger business, however, will probably need at least another employee and a much larger space in which to operate. Other considerations are as follows. Is the woodworking business a sole source of income on a full-time basis? Is the business a part time business? Is the income derived from the business merely extra spending money?

Keeping your business small allows you to focus on your core products. In the first years of your business, it is likely you have very few products available, or you are limiting the commissions completed year over year. In the early stages of a business, this strategy allows you to develop techniques and processes which can be used later when orders or commissions increase. Keeping a business small in the initial years also allows you to develop a good bookkeeping and inventory system. It allows you to develop partnerships with companies where you source your wood, hardware, and other supplies. Improvements in product quality and efficiencies can also be developed over the course of the early years of a woodworking business.

Client feedback from the initial products you deliver can be invaluable to the success of your business. In my experience, a business can quickly grow with both sufficient and targeted marketing, but this should not be a concern early on. In the early stages, it is always best to stay focused on your core products and to maintain quality whether it is furniture, cabinets, or wood products.

Considerations To Expand a Business

Do you have the space for a larger business?

Over the course of my woodworking business experience, I have upgraded from a small shop to a much larger shop. Initially, I began as a hobbyist, progressed to a part-time woodworker, and then explored the challenge of becoming a full-time woodworker. At that time, I realized the need for much more heavy-duty machinery to be able to pre-process rough wood into boards.

It was soon realized that I would also need more shop space since woodworking benches and machinery take up considerable space. The additional benches and large machinery necessitated a larger working space. With this in mind, I invested in a much larger shop with high ceilings, banks of fluorescent lamps, and its own electrical sub-panel. This became a two-storey shop with the bulk of the machinery, dust collectors and equipment in the lower level. The bench room is located on the brighter, well lit upper floor. Separating my machines from my bench area also considerably reduced the likelihood of fine, airborne dust infiltrating my bench areas. As part of the shop design, I also invested in large windows to supply a large amount of natural, ambient light into the workspaces.

The layout of the shop was designed with woodworking in mind. Most machinery is located along the periphery, against the wall or in corners of the shop. The central area of the workshop is reserved for a powerful table saw. The large workbenches, two at this time, are also located away from walls to allow me to work on all sides of the workbenches. I find all these elements to be important in the design of a proper woodworking workshop. Since I currently work alone, the space allocated to this shop area is approximately 650 sq. ft. on each level for a combined area of 1300 sq. ft.

I did plan to expand the business with the possibility of having an employee at some point, but this is no longer necessary. If your current workshop is a confined space without additional available space, this will limit any plans you may have to expand your business. As a first step, you should always calculate the requirements for a larger space when planning for a business expansion. In my own case, an initial basement workshop area was confining and there was no available room for expansion in the home. This shop was located in a part of the basement. My plans for expansion included moving to a larger property and building a dedicated furniture making workshop with many of the characteristics described earlier.

An example of diversification into sculptural work as a product, provided by author. The creation of non-objective art allowed me to diversify into the art market. I would work on these sculptures between commissions to make efficient use of my time and schedule.

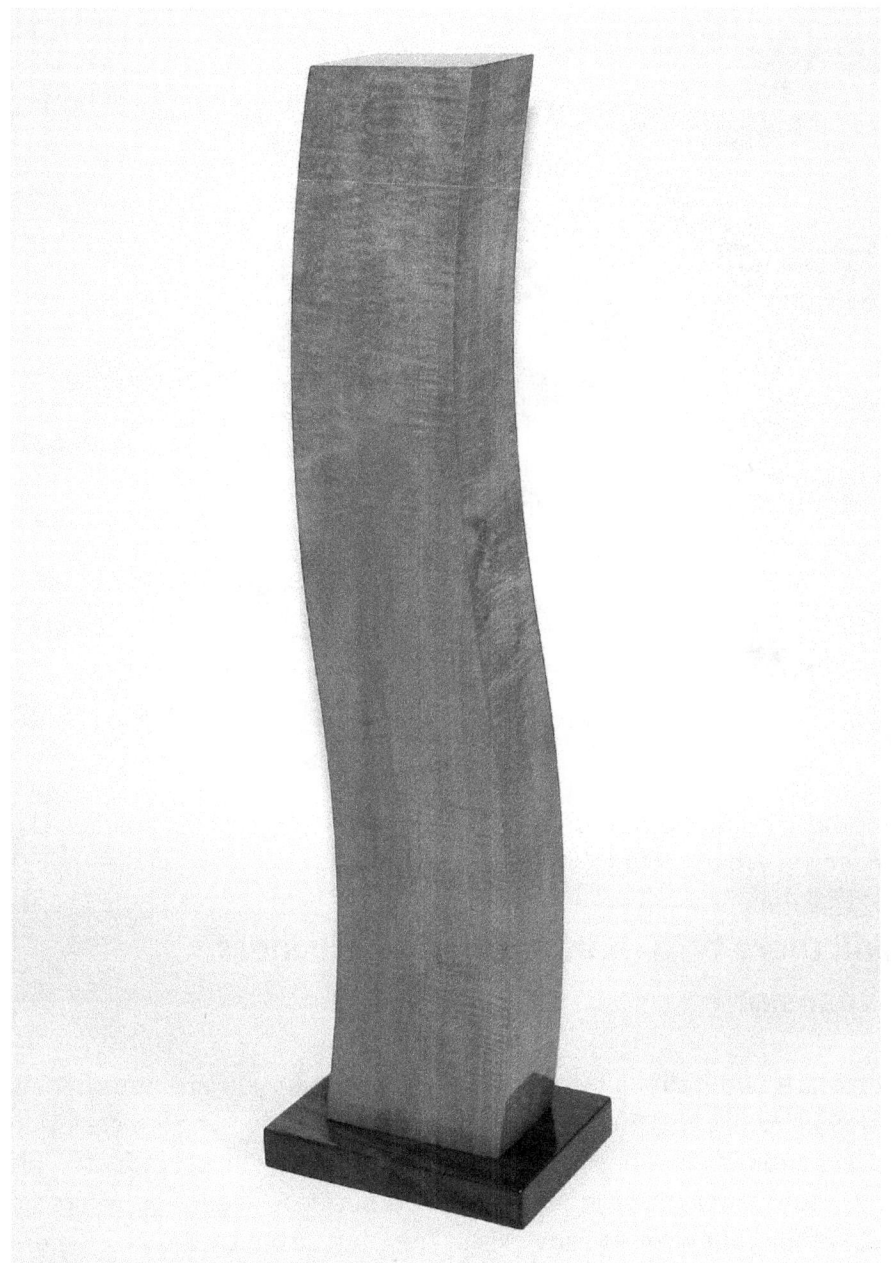

Example of diversification into sculptural work as a product, provided by author. This sculpture incorporates veneered surfaces of figured woods. Work on these sculptures occurs between commissions, making efficient use of my time and schedule.

Another product developed by the author. Hand planes marketed under the White Mountain Toolworks label.

Will there be a market for your business expansion?

There are two paths a business can follow when you are determining whether to expand the business. The first path follows an increase in orders and commissions for furniture, cabinets, or wood products. This is the safest and most logical step for a business expansion since the market for your work already exists. This path also provides an element of confidence in your decision to expand the business. The second path for a business expansion is to take a leap of faith and expand, then ramp up your marketing and advertising to draw in more clients.

This decision involves considerable confidence where it is necessary for you to convince new clients that you are an excellent woodworker, and your work is above par. If you have any doubt that there will not be enough business to warrant an expansion, I would advise to hold off on an expansion and instead diversify into creating other wood products related to your current business.

Do you need to create a larger market for your wood products?

This decision goes hand in hand with what has been mentioned earlier. Expanding your business increases the amount of overhead you will incur. Higher expenses could take the form of higher fixed costs such as increased rent, greater utility costs, and higher insurance premiums. You will need to increase the amount of woodworking business you generate to offset these additional expenses. This formula can be successful although increased advertising and marketing of your business is necessary to bring in more business or commissions.

Often it is preferable to gradually grow a business and keep costs under control. It is far too easy to expand quickly and acquire too much capacity or machinery. It is wise to keep in mind that there will inevitably be a downturn in the business cycle. When a downturn occurs, business will be reduced or possibly come to a standstill. It will be expensive to maintain a large space and machinery at this point.

Are you able to handle the extra business?

Proceeding with a business expansion without the required manpower to offset an increased amount of woodworking can be a problem. An expansion, on the other hand, can be performed in two steps. Initially, you expand the physical shop area either through the lease or rent of a larger space, or alternatively you move to a larger workshop space.

Afterwards, as you gain new business, you can begin to add additional employees. If you proceed with the expansion of both the shop and simultaneously increase your employee count, insufficient orders can be detrimental to the business as overhead costs such as fixed costs and salaries will be higher than your business revenue.

How does an expansion work within your present location?

Although business expansion can be appealing, there can be huge benefits as well as pitfalls to this. Let us begin with the benefits. Market share comes to mind. You presently operate a small woodworking business and clients are beating your door down clamouring for more of your wood products or furniture pieces. This is a good dilemma to be faced with I would say. Therefore, do you keep the woodworking business small or take a leap of faith and expand it to handle the new, guaranteed business. In this case, it is totally dependant on the level of comfort you place in your work-life balance. Making more wood products or furniture and cabinets translates to more time in your workshop. Is this acceptable in your life considering what I discussed earlier in the work-life balance section? Also, can you as an individual woodworker handle the extra work?

Of course, with additional work comes more income which can be a temptation. This formula works until either you cannot handle the extra workload, or you begin to sacrifice the quality of your work. Both these considerations can be detrimental to a business, and I speak from personal experience. Early on I marketed my woodworking business considerably and I sought every avenue available to get the word out that I had a unique product to sell. At first the orders trickled in but a few months later the orders increased considerably and began to overwhelm me.

I was only making jewelry boxes and cigar humidors on a part time basis during this period and had limited time to spend at woodworking. I had to begin pushing completion dates further ahead into the future and ultimately began to refuse orders. This brings us to the pitfalls of expanding a business when you are not completely prepared. When overwhelmed with orders, refusing commissions for products you enjoy creating can be particularly painful. Clients very often leave and never come back, or they take their business to another woodworker. Major opportunities can be lost this way. Your developing reputation as a woodworker can also be negatively affected.

To continue with my personal anecdote, marketing can be a strange experience. If sales and commissions are dismal, the natural inclination is to increase your marketing. This increased emphasis on marketing allows you to explore different avenues of marketing. Even with increased marketing, business can continue to be lacklustre. Then, almost within weeks, business explodes, and you receive many requests for your wood product or commission work. I am pointing out the possibility of a **"lag effect"** which often occurs in advertising and marketing. There is essentially a lag effect in any advertising. Often it is best to gradually increase marketing and advertising to determine what results each form of advertising delivers.

What to do when you realize you are overwhelmed with orders? The natural tendency is to accept the commissions, furniture orders or orders for wood objects. Let us not forget that you are likely the sole person working at making your furniture or wood products. The formula begins to work too well. The logical next step is to either quickly expand or alternatively turn away furniture or wood product orders or commissions. Odds are that you cannot expand quickly enough, and you are not able to handle the new work. Deadlines for commission work are then pushed further and further ahead to where the client finds the wait unreasonable.

Turning away commissions will be the only choice you have unless clients are willing to wait an extended period of time for you to complete their order or complete their commission. I was once faced with this dilemma and needed to turn away as much work as was being received. It broke my heart to do this. This is an example of successful marketing but poor planning!

A factor to consider early on is to implement the possibility of an expansion of your woodworking business in your business plan. It is often wise to consider all the possible directions your business can go in. Having said this, an opportunity is often created by working on a product or a furniture commission and you then stumble upon a new design simply from a nugget of an idea.

Diversification involves the decision to take on work other than the furniture or product you create, or alternatively add to the selection of products you already market. This other product or service you take on can include furniture repair, refinishing of furniture, making outdoor furniture, or creating sculptural work. Another option is to design a clever product or furniture which is easy to produce yet sells very well. This diversification of your business can help you increase the income derived from your woodworking business.

Having a regular, reliable income from your woodworking business is ideal in many ways. A regular income will provide you at the very least with financial security and removes the stress of coping with periods of low sales. Surviving off a woodworking business can be challenging at times. Instead of the usual recourse of working part time elsewhere to pay the bills, it is instead wise to take on some other woodworking related work to provide you with a regular stream of income. The advantages to this are that you can keep your workshop doors open and remain in your place of business. This is especially important if you are a full-time woodworker and have hefty, fixed overhead costs.

Overhead costs such as rent, heating, electric bills, business insurance and other business-related expenses can quickly add up each month and overwhelm a business. It will be a priority to at least cover the fixed overhead costs so your business can remain open. Another advantage of maintaining a small business structure is that it will be much quicker for you to modify your furniture or wood product designs. Production and tooling changes are not obstacles as most of the build process is performed using traditional machinery and hand tools. Jigs are a large part of a woodworker's arsenal. It is both cost-effective and prudent to create a selection of woodworking jigs to help with your woodworking processes and increase the level of repeatability.

A photo of the authors' unique, one-of-a-kind style of contemporary furniture. A showcase cabinet using veneered panels throughout. Veneering is a cost-effective method of acquiring greater yield from a board, specifically figured boards.

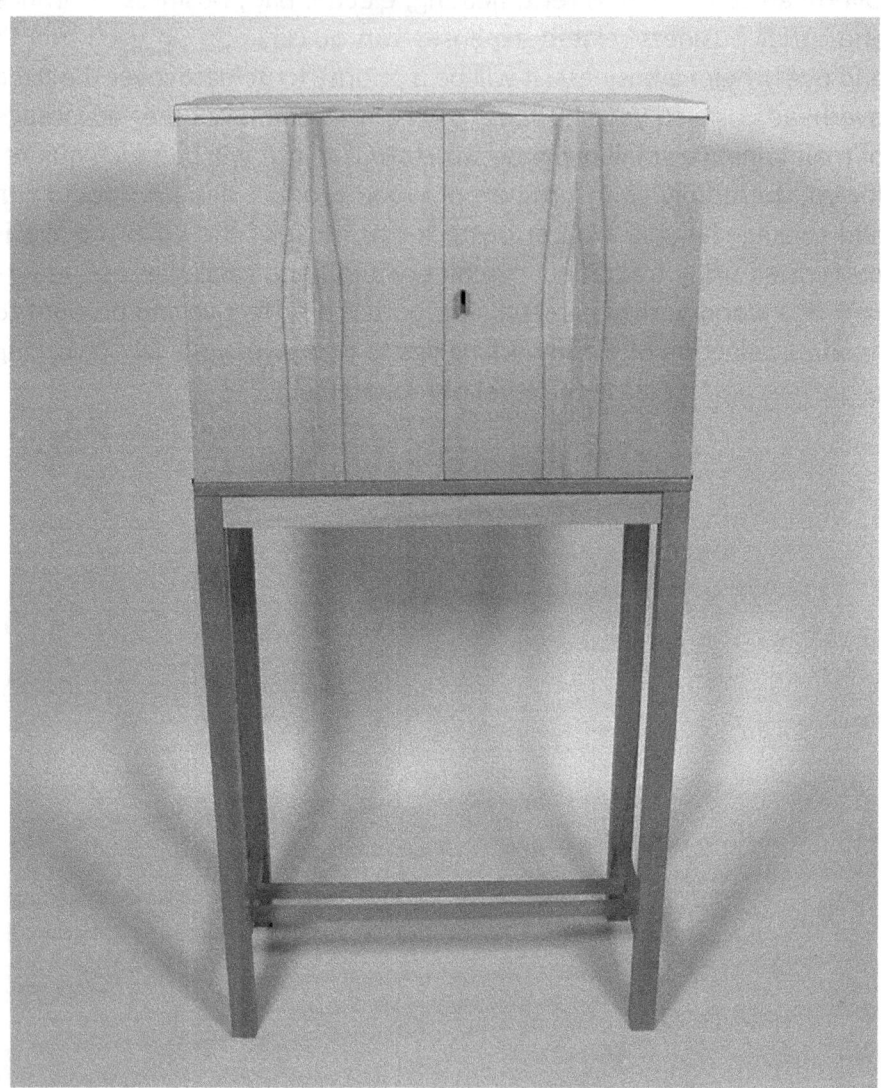

A photo of the authors' unique, one of a kind showcase cabinet using highly figured veneers in the doors. Developing contemporary designs with clean lines is effective in reducing the complexity of creating otherwise complex furniture components. This type of cabinet appeals to a small niche or clientele that appreciates quality, high-end furniture.

Do you need to hire an employee?

Continuing with the expansion and diversification topic. At this crossroad, you can also give thought to the possibility of hiring an employee. I only refer to one additional employee in the following paragraphs since additional employees over and above the first employee follow the same criteria for expansion.

When does it become cost-effective to add an employee to your woodworking business? This depends somewhat on your level of ambition and your drive to succeed. Do you intend to create a much larger woodworking business or are you content as the sole owner and maker of your furniture or wood product? I read of a few instances where woodworkers have expanded and hired employees to assist with increased orders, only to downsize their shop a few years later. The common theme to the downsizing is that the owner finds that he or she is spending much less time building furniture or wood products. Instead, their time is spent administering a complex business and managing employees.

Some woodworkers cope with this as a natural evolution of a business. Others wish to continue hands-on woodworking and control the growth of their woodworking business. I am of the latter mindset; I enjoy designing and making furniture considerably and would never expand my business to where more than one employee is necessary.

It also needs to be understood that with more orders comes increased business-related costs, where each additional employee is a substantial expense. There are different business models which can help you determine how much additional business justifies hiring an additional employee. The extra income derived from this employee is factored into an equation. You will need to offset this increase in expenses with an increase in orders and revenue derived from a larger business employing one or more people.

Having said this, there are a few small woodworking companies that maintain the traditional aspect of making wood products or furniture. These companies have successfully expanded and brought in additional employees. Having examined the structure of these companies, a happy medium appears to have been arrived at. The additional employees and expansion are capped, and the owner and employees are all content at creating wood products or furniture. Perhaps, after many years of making wood products or furniture, the natural progression is to expand a woodworking business. The process of expansion also allows you to train other woodworkers to take charge of the business.

Having a qualified employee as part of your woodworking business can also free you of the more monotonous, repetitive tasks in woodworking. Perhaps there are many repetitive tasks which need to be performed in the creation of your woodwork or furniture designs. Perhaps your style of woodworking involves multiples or small batches of similar products with interchangeable components produced using jigs. This work can be both repetitive and monotonous at times. A qualified employee can accomplish these tasks while freeing you up to work on new designs, handcrafting the detail work of your furniture, or investing time in the administrative aspects of your business.

This is a path I wish to explore further as my business increases. Being a hands-on person, I like to be part of the design + build process. I like to maintain my hand tool skills and all the expertise I have gained over the years. Through the hiring of an employee, I can focus on these aspects of woodworking instead of having to do everything myself. I can task the employee with more monotonous processes, the ones that I no longer enjoy doing or have little time to perform. This is a topic to consider in your own woodworking business.

Demi-lune table is a contemporary design, courtesy of author. This table design incorporates metal and wood as well as highly figured wood. The table was designed for the prestigious **art09** show. It was recommended to have my latest and boldest work as part of the show. The demi-lune table is an example of "out of the box" thinking where design takes precedence over function.

Prototypes of a new hi-back contemporary styled lounge chair designed by the author and introduced at **IDS15** in January 2015. The prototypes have lightening holes installed to reduce the weight of the lounge chair. Assembly consists of a single bolt and a few small screws to attach the back to the frame. This is an example of a flat-pack furniture design.

The completed hi-back lounge chair with a walnut base and top grain leather seating and innovative X-pattern frame construction. The lounge chair features a unique knock-down design to allow the components to be flat-pack shipped. ©2015 Marc Lavoie - Courtesy Marc Lavoie Photography.

Technology in Woodworking

Woodworking processes, techniques and tools have remained static over the past decades. Having said this, technology has entered the world of woodworking. As in almost every other type of manufacturing, technological changes are slowly creeping into the field of woodworking. Technological innovations were developed to address the need for increasing productivity in furniture and cabinet factories while utilizing less manpower. Large scale woodworking operations are far removed from the small woodworking business I have discussed in this book. Today, many small woodworking businesses operate using traditional processes, but they are quickly discovering and embracing new CNC technology.

Technology designed for large factory operations is filtering down to smaller woodworking shops. Technology in the form of automated saws and CNC machinery has become affordable for the small shop. Technology is quickly being adopted where repeated processing of panels is necessary. Typically, a panel for furniture or a cabinet requires several cuts, many drilled holes and dado or rabbet grooves. CNC machines can perform these operations unattended all-day long. CNC machines operate in 3-axis, X and Y and Z (up and down).

Each axis is controlled by software allowing a cutter to make 3-D movements. The cutter is typically a router with a variety of high capacity, specialized cutting bits available. A typical medium sized woodworking CNC machine with tooling is shown on the next page. A sizeable investment is necessary in acquiring a complex CNC machine. These machines are ideal at repetitive work in a factory or intermediate sized shop setting. The factory could be large or small, the business owner will need to determine if a CNC machine is warranted. One immediate advantage is the need for fewer employees.

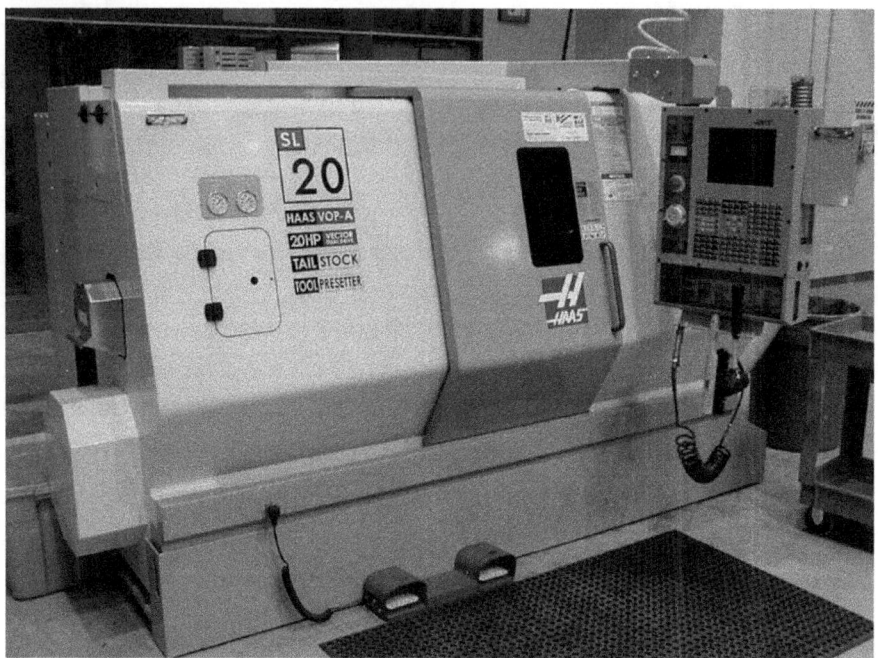

"Small CNC Turning Center" by Nathaniel C. Sheetz. Licensed under CC BY-SA 3.0 via Wikimedia

Instead of using a tablesaw to cut boards or panels, a drill press to make holes and a router to make grooves into the panel; a CNC machine combines all three of these operations and is also capable of more complex cuts. All movements on a CNC machine are guided through specialized software which, over time, is becoming simpler to use. Automated saws with auto feed and precision ripping and crosscut operations are now affordable for the small shop.

This automated machinery enables the shop owner to spend more time designing furniture and cabinets. It also allows a small shop to have fewer employees since mundane boring and cutting operations can now be performed by automated machines. The reluctance in accepting these machines has been overcome and they are now being embraced in the woodworking industry.

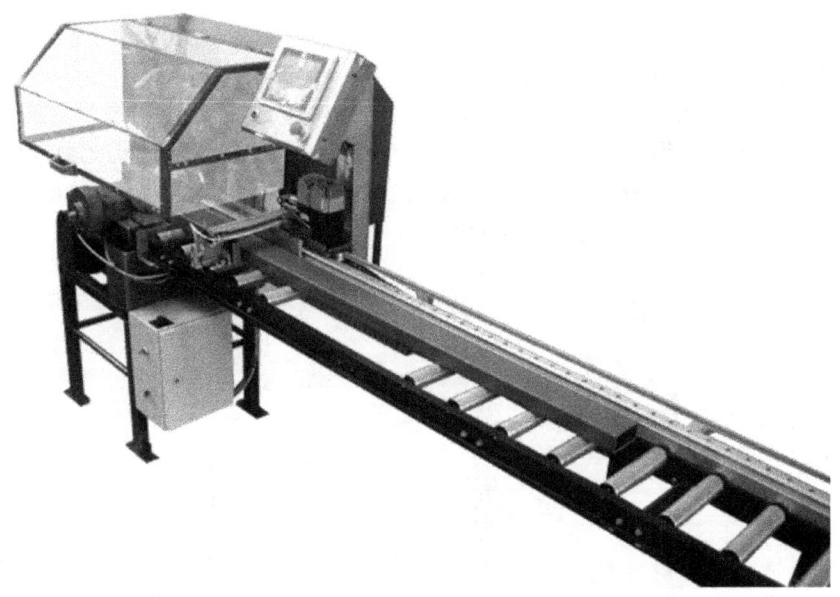

The choice is up to the small woodworking shop owner. Do they continue to manually process panels for furniture or cabinets, or do they embrace technology in the form of CNC machinery? The affordability of CNC has become an enticing reason to purchase this new technology. Often, the expense of the CNC machine is largely offset by the reduced number of employee's necessary to operate a woodworking shop. Small woodworking shops, typically kitchen cabinet makers, are embracing CNC to both increase productivity and remain competitive.

CNC machines also allow a small shop to bring in other work during slow periods. CNC machines are designed to run all day so there are many hours available to process panels from other shops. The extra revenue gained from this can be the deciding factor to whether a small woodworking shop survives. Software designed to operate CNC machinery can be beneficial to a small shop in other ways. The software can be used to convert computer generated designs to the special code used to operate CNC machinery.

The design software (CAD) can also be used independently to rapidly draw and render furniture or cabinets to precise dimensions. Using CAD, the dimensions can easily be modified and updated throughout the furniture design. This step is a great timesaver. The furniture or cabinet design can also be rendered in 3-D so it can be rotated and visualized at different angles. A better perspective of the design can thus be viewed. This contrasts with tedious line drawing on paper with orthographic and perspective views.

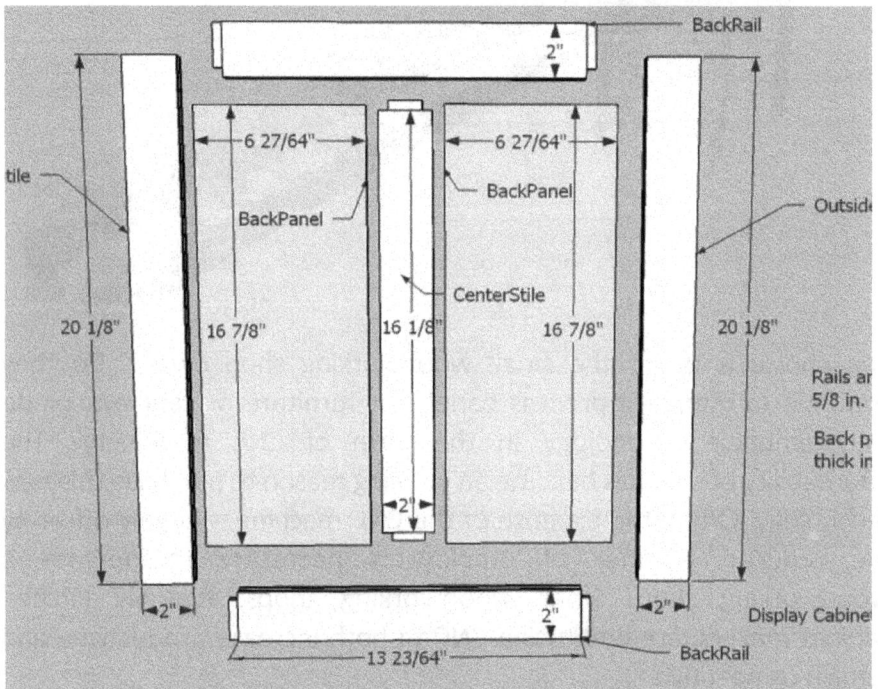

Using CAD to draw the components of a back panel for a cabinet, courtesy of author. The precise measurements allow the build of the cabinet to proceed quickly. Components can be individually created or created in multiples or small batches.

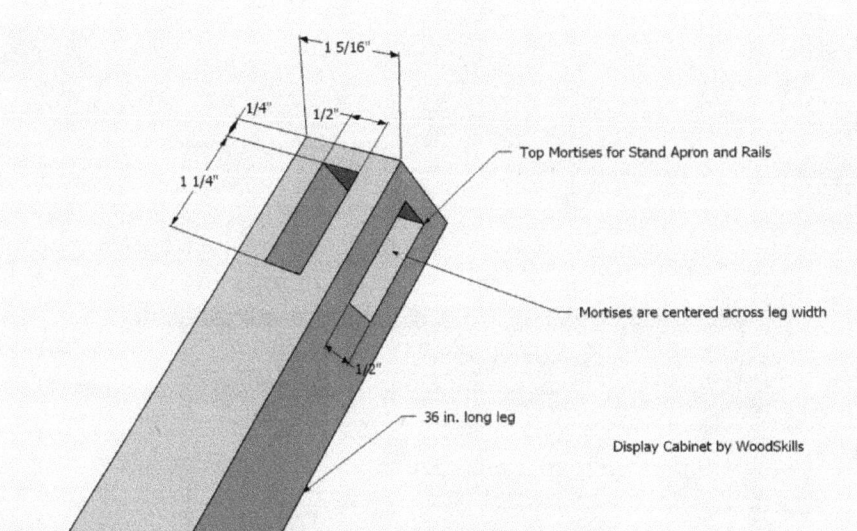

Use of CAD to provide 3-D detail of the joinery used in a component of furniture. The precise measurements can be quickly transferred to furniture components.

Both conventional pencil drawings and CAD (Computer Aided Design) software are currently used in my woodworking business to both draw and flesh designs out. I typically begin with a pencil drawing and progress to a CAD drawing once the dimensions have been input into the software program.

The CAD software allows me to quickly make changes, add or remove components and use a library of other components in the design. Rendering of the design in CAD allows me to view a furniture design from all angles in 3-D. Color is also added to the different components to be able to distinguish them from one another. Basic CAD software (Sketchup) is freely available, allowing you to learn about CAD. If you so choose, you can progress to more advanced CAD software after becoming familiar with the basic concept and process of CAD design.

Side table designed and rendered using CAD software, courtesy of author. Using CAD software allows design changes to be quickly made and rendered without the need for re-drawing the design on paper. Considerable time can be therefore saved in the design process. Time which can instead be spent at woodworking.

Social Media for Woodworkers

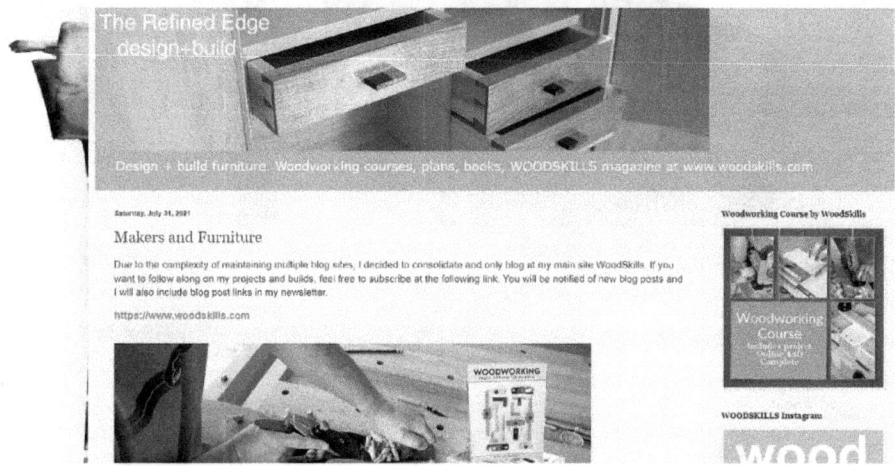

Refined Edge Blog, chronicling my journey into furniture making

In recent years there has been an explosion of social media platforms that can bring awareness to your furniture making business. The most popular and widespread media platforms include Twitter, Facebook, Linkedin, Instagram, YouTube, and Pinterest. The next pages identify the social media platforms I use most often, and those that have the greatest potential for exposure of your business. Consequently, I have embraced social media as an effective marketing tool for business.

The original social media platform, **Facebook,** has evolved to include an option specifically to promote business. The Facebook Page option is designed with business in mind. A Facebook Business page is separate from your personal page but is easily accessed through your Facebook profile. For example, a personal user on Facebook can create a business page and have it available to view while logged into Facebook. This significantly reduces the steps necessary to access and update your Facebook page. In other words, one-stop shopping. It is relatively straightforward to create a Facebook Business page and populate it with critical business information.

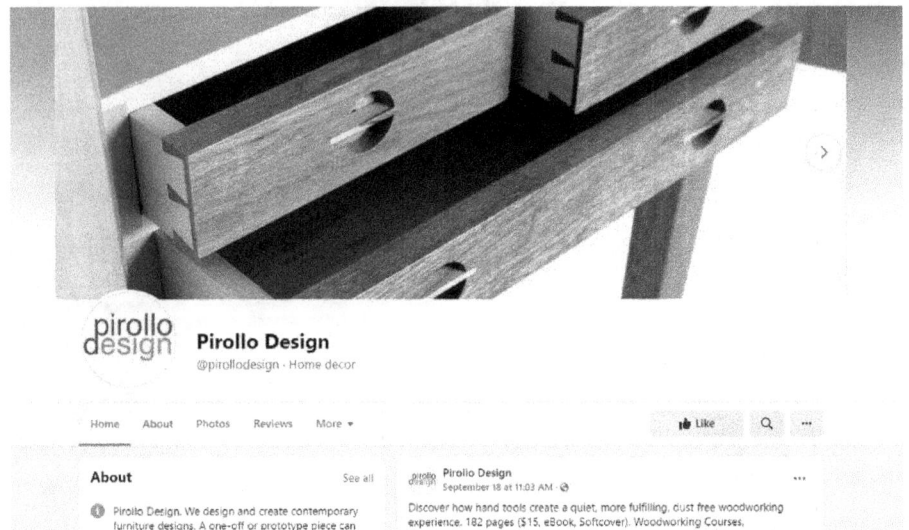
Facebook Business page (Pirollo Design)

The Facebook Business page then takes on a life of its own and with clever marketing will draw clients to your business. Facebook Business pages are also used as a peer-to-peer networking tool to discover other businesses to aid in marketing your business. It resembles a reciprocal arrangement with another business. I consider this cross-pollination. Other businesses, local and distant, will find and seek you for business-to business activity. Posts on a Facebook Business page include new product announcements, new furniture designs, and positive reviews of your business.

Static information on a Facebook Business page includes your business location, business hours, a website link, contact info, and specific information about your business.

A feature that a business account provides is advertising in the form of promotional post boosts as well as dedicated advertising campaigns. Facebook ad campaigns are set up to target the demographic most likely to purchase your work. The ads are published in-line with regular posts and are visible when people scroll through their newsfeed.

If both targeting and focused interests have been strategically set up in a Facebook ad campaign, the likelihood of a response to your ad increases. Ad campaigns can be set up as either CPC (Cost Per Click) or Post views. The CPC strategy directs a person to your website or wherever your work is sold. Post views instead present your post to as many viewers as possible, ideal for branding of your furniture designs. In optimal circumstances, your Facebook post will be shared by a Facebook viewer. Sharing compounds post visibility and is invaluable to getting the word out of your woodworking business.

Twitter is another of the wave of new social media platforms that can expose your business to tens of thousands of potential clients. By regularly posting and engaging with other Twitter businesses and followers, your posts will be seen by significantly more people. Being active on social media is key to being successful on any of these social media platforms. Twitter is historically one of the earliest social media platforms and had grown exponentially since its inception. Twitter users. Twitter users engage with each other.

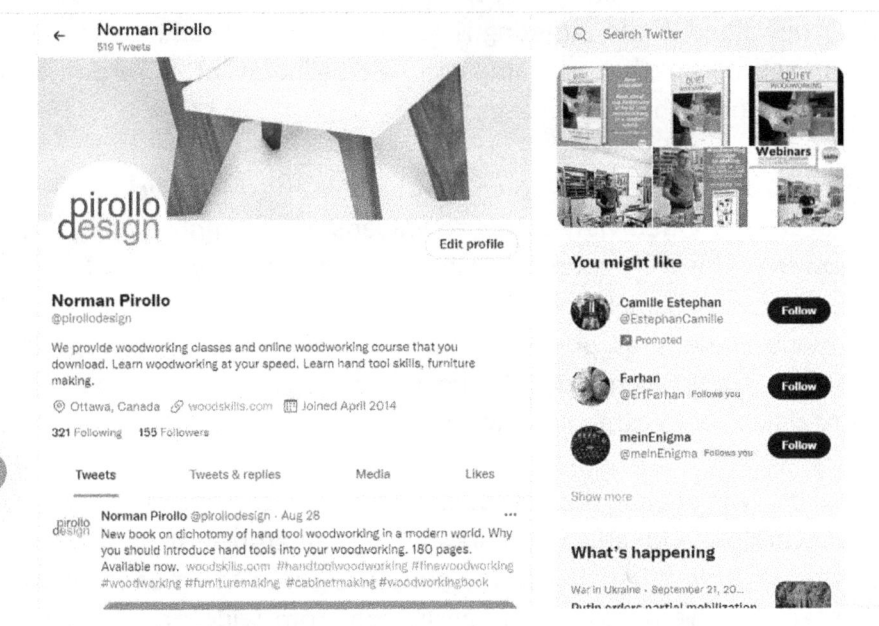

Snapshot of Twitter account (Pirollo Design)

It is possible to join Twitter either on a personal basis or set yourself up as a business. A business account provides the most benefit to your business. A Twitter business account can tap into hundreds of thousands of people with similar interests. Each instance of a Twitter post acquires Likes, Comments and Retweets that in turn increase engagement of your post and raise its ranking. Through an advanced algorithm, a higher-ranking Twitter post is then served to more followers. It is this cascading exposure that will benefit your business.

Twitter posts include text with static images or a video. Hashtags included in your Twitter post strategically target certain niches. Hashtags have a life of their own and facilitate a search for a category of post. For example, an often-used hashtag applied to my posts on all social media platforms is **#woodworking**. This hashtag, one of many relevant hashtags, will increase the possibility of being noticed by a Twitter user applying the search term **woodworking**. Another feature of a Twitter business account is advertising. Twitter ad campaigns can be set up to target the demographic most likely to purchase your work. The ads are in-line with regular posts when people scroll through their newsfeed. If the targeting is accurate and focused interests have been set up in the ad campaign, a likelihood of a response or engagement to the ad increases.

Ad campaigns can be set up with either PPC (Pay Per Click) or Tweet engagement. Video views, App downloads or to simply increase your followers. The PPC strategy will drive traffic to your website or wherever your work is sold. A tweet engagement displays your post to as many viewers as possible and increases brand awareness. In a Twitter ad campaign, you set the daily budget and duration of the campaign. The ad campaign runs continually until the expiry date.

Detailed Twitter analytics are available to monitor response to your ad. Monetization and affiliate marketing are features of social media platforms such as Twitter. Many people tap into the monetization of Twitter and the recurring money gained from widespread exposure and engagement of their posts.

An ideal monetization situation is when a Twitter user clicks a link to your website and makes a purchase. However, maintaining a social media effort will take valuable time away from your business. You will need to determine how much of your time to allocate to social media so the impact to your core business is minimal. Another option is to task other people with social media savvy with marketing your business, although this is the pricier option. In my own business, I handle the social media posts and the marketing campaigns. Also important is the return on investment of a social media ad campaign. If insufficient results are received, it becomes necessary to either modify the campaign or to seek alternate forms of advertising. If your business caters to a strictly local market, local newspapers, magazines, and word of mouth are perhaps a better option.

Linkedin was an early social media adopter on the Internet. It is the most professional and business oriented of the social media platforms. A presence on Linkedin is almost expected of a business or career professional today. Linkedin is used mainly for professional networking between its members. Career professionals can share their successes, seek new opportunities, and make it known that they are in the market for new career challenges. Linkedin also caters to businesses and has become an excellent platform to make announcements or introduce new products. Although it is not expected for individuals or businesses to post on Linkedin as regularly as other social media platforms, the weight and value of each post id substantially more effective. Consequently, the quality of posts on Linkedin is greater than on other social media platforms.

Linkedin membership is freely available, although the method of creating and building your social network differs somewhat from other platforms. To become a Linkedin member, you create a profile which includes relevant information including your profile (bio), CV, accomplishments, and education. As well, your current and past employment is noted.

As woodworker or furniture maker, this is where you indicate that you are self-employed at your own business. Once you have become a Linkedin member, the Linkedin strategy is to request from other members to join your social media network and form a connection with you and your business. This concept applies to both individuals and businesses.

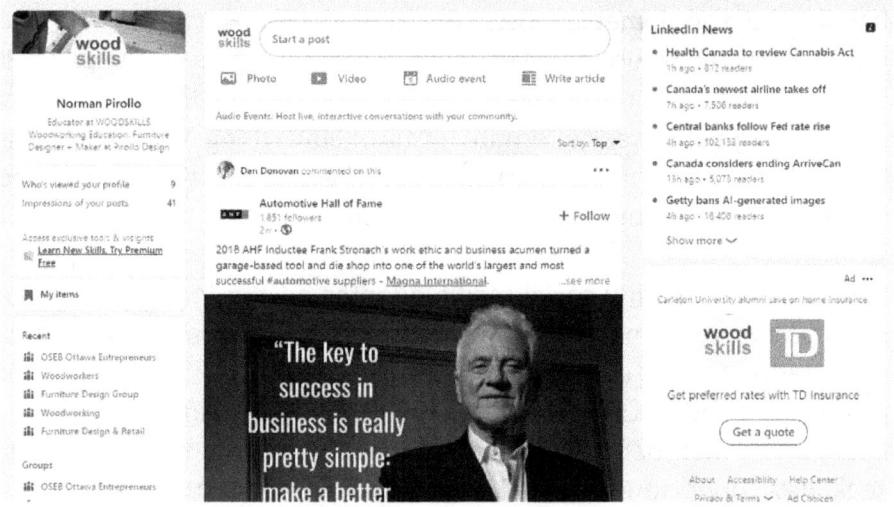
Snapshot of Linkedin account (Norman Pirollo)

There are nested levels of participation in your social network where each person in your network is considered a connection. Your network comprises 1st degree, 2nd degree, and 3rd degree connections. A higher ranking or 1st degree connection indicates a close connection to an individual invited into your respective network.

A 2nd degree connection is a member connected to your 1st degree connection. A 3rd degree connection or individual has a connection with your 2nd degree connection. This cascading concept allows you to cultivate relationships with other Linkedin members that have a vested interest in your type of business. Rather than simply acquiring followers as on other social media platforms, Linkedin prefers that you select and foster a relationship with a smaller but more relevant community of members.

The Linkedin emphasis is on quality of contacts rather than the sheer number of followers. Since Linkedin focuses on professionalism, the posts are centered on successes, career changes, business opportunities, new product announcements, awards, and recognition.

As a furniture maker, Linkedin is an ideal medium to share a new furniture design or woodworking products. Individual Linkedin users can follow businesses and individuals. Linkedin also features groups you can join or even create your own group. As a member of a Linkedin group, you and your business will be in even closer proximity to prospective clients. As a furniture maker, Linkedin enables you to develop a substantial network of people interested in your work and acquiring your work. Business opportunities can be created and developed through Linkedin. Nurturing relationships with other businesses can assist with outsourcing certain processes or components of your furniture. For example, some furniture makers would rather not finish their furniture pieces and instead outsource this task to professional finishers. Another example is to combine metal and wood in your furniture pieces. You can seek businesses to outsource fabrication or powder coating of the metal components. Other businesses can also seek you out to create furniture related opportunities. Linkedin members are very reciprocal in this regard.

Instagram is a relatively new kid on the social media block. Instagram began as a photo sharing platform and still is. At the time of this writing, Instagram has also embraced video in its platform. Video posts in the form of stories and reels of varying durations can now be posted. Their duration is limited to several seconds or in many cases minutes. Stores and reels are very effective at engaging with viewers. You can demonstrate a new technique or process through video more effectively than through images. The traditional post with only images continues to form a large part of Instagram posts and is extremely effective at increasing the number of followers (people) to your account. This essentially increases your social media exposure as a woodworker or furniture maker.

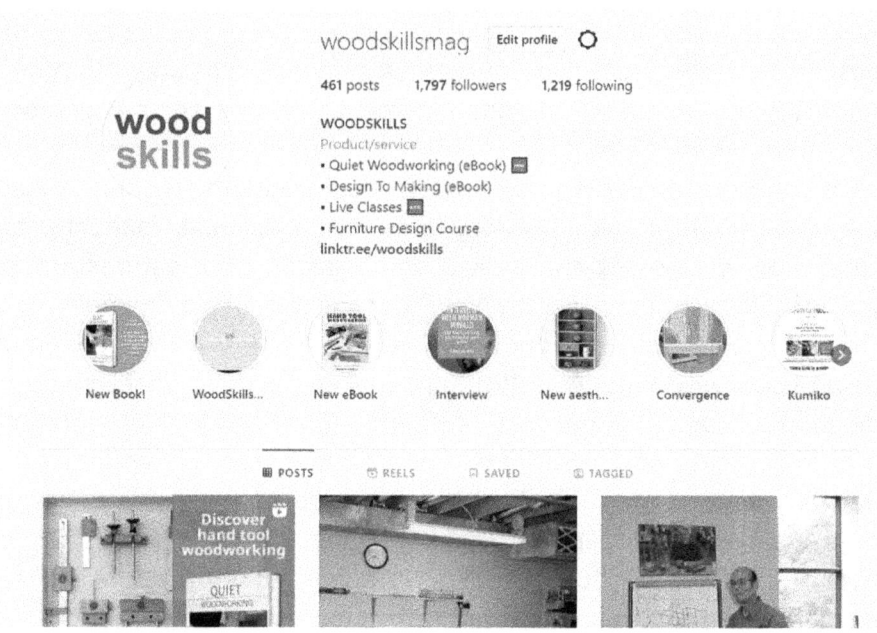

Snapshot of Instagram Account (WoodSkills)

Instagram accounts used to be strictly personal although the recent addition of a business account option has changed this. It is now possible to change a personal account to a professional or business account. Instagram business accounts have the advantage of providing analytics to the account owner. Through analytics, the engagement and exposure a post receives is available through charts and figures.

Analytics is a valuable to a business owner. A business owner can determine the demographic that is viewing and engaging with their posts. They can also determine what time of day and weekdays the posts are most active with engagement. Through regular posting and engagement with your Instagram followers and other Instagram accounts, more viewers see your posts. The posts move up in ranking as a result. Being active is key to success on any social media platform.

Instagram is a relative newcomer to social media and has grown exponentially in recent years. An Instagram post acquires Likes, Comments and Shares. Each action increases engagement of the post and raises its ranking. Through complex algorithms, a highly ranked Instagram post is served to even more followers. It is this cascading exposure that benefits a business the most.

Another feature a business account provides is access to advertising. Instagram ad campaigns are a recent addition and are set up to target the demographic most likely to purchase your work or service. The ads are in-line with regular posts when viewers scroll through their feeds.

If the Instagram targeting is correctly performed and focused interests have been set up in an ad campaign, the likelihood of response to the ad increases. Ad campaigns can be set up as either PPC (Pay Per Click) or set up for post engagements, video views, or simply to increase your followers. The PPC strategy drives traffic to your website or wherever your work is sold. Post engagement instead presents your post to as many viewers as possible, increasing the exposure received and subsequent branding of your business and products. As of this writing, Instagram does not offer a monetization option, although it will be available in the future according to industry insiders. Posting and reading posts consumes an inordinate amount of time that is time away from your business. You will need to determine how much of your time to allocate to social media. This is so it does not significantly interfere from your core woodworking or furniture making business.

YouTube is another popular social media platform to promote your business and to develop a following. The premise of YouTube is the sharing of videos. It is the earliest large-scale video sharing service available on the Internet. Millions of members and viewers connect with YouTube daily. A member can create an account and a channel associated with it. The channel should have a unique, easily remembered name.

The channel is then populated with videos you create. YouTube is ubiquitous and widely recognized as the go to source for instructional videos on wide-ranging topics. The caveat to YouTube's popularity is that videos are mostly home spun. There is considerable chaff to sort through to find a gem or quality video from by a knowledgeable person. It becomes important to identify the YouTube makers that are familiar with the subject they demonstrate.

If one needs to quickly learn about a particular topic or product, YouTube is a good choice for a video explaining the topic. For in-depth understanding there is always the risk that it is not presented by a knowledgeable person. In other words, you get what you pay for. YouTube is a large, well-known platform for sharing videos but not strong at developing business relationships. As a furniture maker, YouTube offers the potential to demonstrate your furniture making techniques and skills. YouTube is an effective platform to host videos describing the wood products or furniture pieces you create. As well, you can profile yourself as a woodworker or furniture maker and promote your business in the form of videos. I regularly post videos on my YouTube channel that describe various techniques used in my furniture making or a new product announcement.

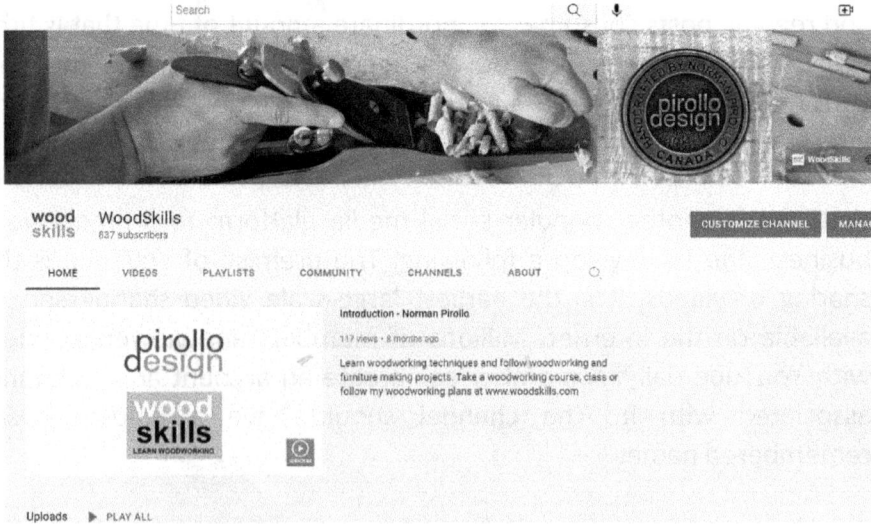

Snapshot of YouTube account (WoodSkills)

Through YouTube videos, you can demonstrate the joinery you use, your furniture making philosophy, and the processes you follow to create your furniture pieces. Proficiency in creating quality videos is a criteria, although with the current crop of video editing software, this task has become straightforward and simpler. Through basic editing, videos can now be created on smartphones, tablets, desktop computers and then transferred directly to You Tube.

The choice is yours whether you wish to create videos that are professional in appearance or to simply post videos on the go. The latter choice is often the best choice since video editing is time consuming. This takes valuable time away from your core business. My advice here is to maintain good video quality and to make editing simple enough to not impact your core woodworking or furniture making. Once your YouTube channel is established, playlists of video selections can be added. This feature allows you to organize and present videos by topic.

Playlists make it easier for a viewer of your channel to select the relevant videos they choose to watch. The YouTube platform has a highly regarded search feature to search through the mammoth YouTube repository of videos on any topic. Apply optimized keywords to your video description and the search function enables a viewer to quickly find your channel and videos. YouTube viewers can also comment on your videos allowing you to engage with the viewer and increase exposure of your channel. Videos can also be shared among viewers. Through sharing, the potential for your video to be seen increases substantially. If a viewer likes your video and channel, they can then subscribe to your channel.

When you add a video to your channel, your subscribers are automatically notified of your latest video. Views to your videos and channel increase by having the number of subscribers to your channel grow. The monetization option is available on the YouTube platform.

Once your subscriber number surpasses a certain mark, namely 100k subscribers, you have the potential of earning money through your videos. The monetisation is in the form of compensation for number of views per video as well as the length of viewing per video. The takeaway here is to embrace social media and use it to market and publicize your woodworking business.

Pinterest is a social media website and platform that allows users to organize and share images and videos from around the Internet. Pinterest is essentially an online pin (image) board, a modern take on bookmarking and collecting images. It also serves as a discovery engine for popular topics including woodworking and furniture making. The premise is to either create or save a pin to a board on your Pinterest account. Followers to your Pinterest account can then find the pin through the boards you created and (pin) or share it on their own board. This enables the original pin to propagate on the Internet and direct people to your web site. The brings awareness to your business.

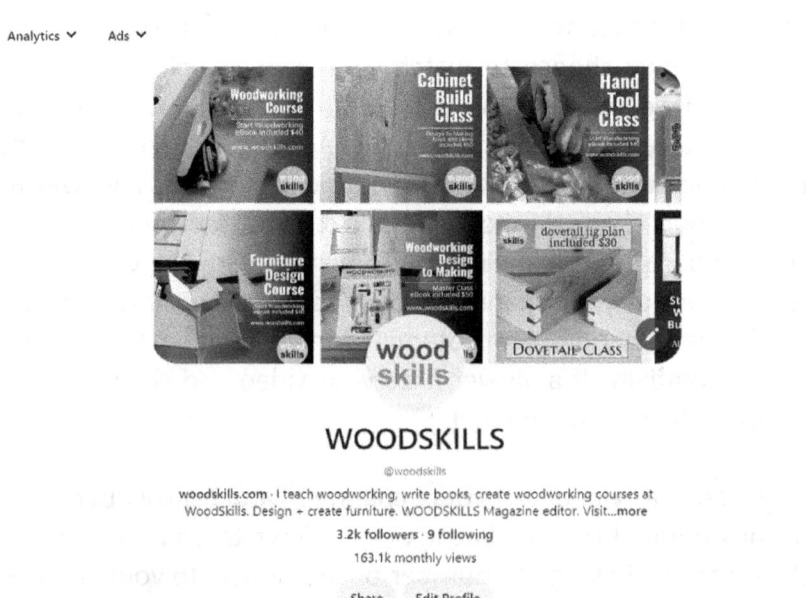

Snapshot of Pinterest account (WoodSkills)

Conclusion

I hope you have enjoyed this book and it has motivated and inspired you to move forward with your woodworking business. The best years of my life have been while self-employed at my woodworking businesses. I have often told myself that if the business fails, a return to the workforce could easily be made with a new set of skills. Reciting this has given me peace of mind and has thankfully never occurred.

The author maintains a blog of his woodworking which chronicles furniture created in his studio at:

http://refinededge.blogspot.ca

http://pirollodesign.com/blog/

The author offers online woodworking instruction through:

https://www.woodskills.com

For daily posts about furniture builds and workshop activity:

Instagram: **https://www.instagram.com/woodskillsmag**

www.ingramcontent.com/pod-product-compliance
Lightning Source LLC
Chambersburg PA
CBHW070458090426
42735CB00012B/2596